WASHINGTON

Rock
Minerals

A Field Guide to the Evergreen and Bea

Dan R. Lynch & Bob Lynch

Adventure Publications
Cambridge, Minnesota

Dedication

To Nancy Lynch, wife of Bob and mother of Dan, for her love and continued support of our book projects.

And to Julie Kirsch, Dan's wife, for her love and patience.

Acknowledgments

Thanks to the following for providing specimens and/or information: Arlene Handley, Haven Andrist, Phil Andrist and Eugene Mueller

Photography by Dan R. Lynch

Cover and book design by Jonathan Norberg

Edited by Brett Ortler

15 14 13 12 11 10 9

Washington & Oregon Rocks & Minerals
Copyright © 2012 by Dan R. Lynch and Bob Lynch
Published by Adventure Publications
An imprint of AdventureKEEN
310 Garfield Street South
Cambridge, Minnesota 55008
(800) 678-7006
www.adventurepublications.net
Printed in China
ISBN 978-1-59193-293-2 (pbk.)

Table of Contents

Introduction

Washington and Oregon are two of the premier areas for rock and mineral collecting in the western United States. The two states are home to dozens of highly collectible minerals, many of which are easily accessible. They are also home to some minerals that can't be found anywhere else in the country.

This geological treasure trove is the result of an incredible amount of geological activity in both states. Of course, when most people think of the geology of Washington and Oregon, they think of the awesome power displayed by the eruption of Mount St. Helens in 1980. But the towering volcanoes of the High Cascades are only one part of the area's fascinating story. From the rugged ocean beaches in the west to the rolling hills of the eastern portions of both states, Washington and Oregon are replete with natural landmarks that are evidence of the area's incredible geological past. By showing you how to recognize and identify the natural wonders just beneath your feet, this book will show you the much quieter (but equally amazing) side of Washington and Oregon.

Important Terms and Definitions

Books about geology are not always easy for amateur rock collectors to understand. In order to make this book intuitive for novices yet still useful for experienced collectors, when we include technical geological terms in the text, we "translate" them immediately by providing a brief definition. In this way, amateurs can learn some of the more important terminology relevant to the hobby in an easy, straightforward manner. Of course, all of the geology-related terms are also defined in the glossary found at the back of this book.

If you're entirely new to rock and mineral collecting, there are a few very important terms that you should understand, not only before you begin researching and collecting minerals, but even before you read this book. Many people go hunting for rocks and minerals without knowing the difference between the two. The difference is simple: a **mineral** is formed from the crystallization (solidification) of a single element, or more commonly a chemical compound (a combination of elements). For example, silicon dioxide, a chemical compound consisting of the elements silicon and oxygen, crystallizes to form quartz, the most abundant mineral on earth. In contrast, a **rock** is a mass of solid material containing a mixture of many different minerals. Pure minerals exhibit definite and testable characteristics, such as a specific hardness and a distinct repeatable shape. Rocks do not, and vary greatly because of the various minerals contained within them. This can make it more difficult for amateurs to identify rocks.

Many of the most important terms apply only to minerals and their crystals. A **crystal** is a solid object with a distinct shape and a repeating atomic structure that is created by the solidification of a chemical compound. In other words, when different elements come together, they form a chemical compound that takes on a very specific shape when it hardens. For example, the mineral galena is lead sulfide, a chemical compound consisting of lead and sulfur. When it **crystallizes**, or solidifies, it takes the shape of a cube. A "repeating atomic structure" means that when a crystal grows, it builds upon itself. If you compared two crystals of galena, one an inch long and the other a foot long, they would have the same identical cubic shape. In contrast, if a mineral is not found in a well-crystallized form but rather as a solid, rough chunk, it is said to be **massive**. If a mineral typically forms **massively**, it will frequently be found in irregular pieces, or masses, rather than as well-formed crystals.

Cleavage is the property of some minerals to break in a particular way when carefully struck. As solid as minerals may seem, many have planes of weakness within them that derive from a mineral's internal crystal structure. These points of weakness are called **cleavage planes** and it is along these planes that some minerals will **cleave**, or separate, when struck. For example, galena has cubic cleavage, and even the most irregular piece of galena will fragment into perfect cubes if carefully broken.

Luster is the intensity with which a mineral reflects light. The luster of a mineral is described by comparing its reflectivity to that of a known material. A mineral with "glassy" luster (also called a "vitreous" luster), for example, is similar to the "shininess" of glass. The distinction of a "dull" luster is reserved for the most poorly reflective minerals, while "adamantine" describes the most brilliant. Minerals with a "metallic" luster clearly resemble metal and this can be a very diagnostic trait. But determining a mineral's luster is a subjective experience, so not all observers will necessarily agree, especially when it comes to less obvious lusters, such as "waxy" or "greasy."

When minerals form, they do so on or in rocks. Therefore, it is important to understand the distinction between the different types of rocks if you hope to find a specific mineral. **Igneous** rocks form as a result of volcanic activity and originate from magma, lava, or volcanic ash. **Magma** is hot, molten rock buried deep within the earth and it can take an extremely long time for it to cool and form rock. **Lava**, on the other hand, is molten rock that reaches the earth's surface, where it cools and solidifies into rock very rapidly. A few igneous rocks are made of **volcanic ash**, which forms when explosive, gas-rich volcanic eruptions pulverize rock into dust that settles into large masses to form rock. **Sedimentary** rocks typically form at the bottoms of lakes and oceans when sediment compacts and solidifies into layered masses. This sediment can contain organic matter as well as weathered fragments or grains from broken-down igneous rocks, metamorphic rocks, or other sedimentary rocks. Finally, **metamorphic** rocks develop when igneous or sedimentary rocks are subjected to heat and pressure within the earth. As a result, their mineral composition and appearance changes.

A Brief Overview of the Geology of Washington and Oregon

When looking at the geology of any area, certain features stand out not only as prominent landmarks, but also as important yardsticks of the state's geological past. Washington and Oregon are fairly unique in that they share most of their major landforms, such as the rugged, lush Pacific Coast in the west, the relatively flat and dry Columbia Plateau in the east, and the towering volcanoes of the Cascade Mountain Range in between. The stories of these areas are not quite as complex as they may initially seem, and each begins with the slow yet powerful movement of the Earth's crust.

Tectonic Plates and the Ancient Pacific Northwest

The Earth consists of distinct layers that vary in terms of composition and mechanics. The outermost portion, which includes the ground we walk upon, is a very thin, rigid layer known as the crust. The crust rests atop a solid layer, called the lithosphere, which is much larger, ranging from 60–120 miles thick. The lithosphere, and therefore the crust above it, is broken up into enormous segments called tectonic plates. Like boats on water, these plates float on a deeper layer of flowing molten rock called the asthenosphere. The constantly moving nature of the asthenosphere causes the tectonic plates above it to shift and move, making them crack, spread and smash into each other. On a short-term basis, this movement results in earthquakes and volcanic eruptions, but over millennia it can build mountains, oceans and entire continents.

Washington and Oregon are a prime example of how much the interactions between tectonic plates can alter the landscape. Approximately one billion years ago, the Pacific Ocean extended to the western border of modern-day Idaho. At that point, Washington and Oregon existed only as a coastal plain of sediment collecting on North America's western shore. Things weren't quick to change, either; it remained this way for a few hundred million years. But tectonic plates are always moving, and the plate underneath North America (appropriately named the North American Plate) was slowly crawling westward. At the same time, the plate that underlies the Pacific Ocean (called the Pacific Plate) was moving eastward. Eventually, they collided.

When tectonic plates converge, several things can happen, but the exact interaction is determined by the type of crust above them. Continental plates reside under landmasses, and the crust above them is composed mostly of a 20- to 30-mile thick layer of granite (a light-colored and coarse-grained igneous rock). Oceanic plates, on the other hand, are situated beneath earth's oceans and are topped with a thin, 3- to 4-mile thick layer of oceanic crust composed of basalt (a dense, fine-grained igneous rock).

When two continental plates smash into each other, the thick masses of light granite are thrusted upwards, forming hills and mountains. When a dense, heavy, basalt-topped oceanic plate meets a continental plate, the oceanic plate is driven downward as the lighter continental plate slides over it. This process is called subduction.

During plate subduction, an enormous trench forms at the boundary where the oceanic plate is pushed beneath the continental plate, and large amounts of sediment accumulate in the gap. As the oceanic plate is pushed beneath the continental plate, it travels downward at a shallow angle. When the oceanic crust reaches the molten asthenosphere and itself melts, some of that molten rock is forced upwards.

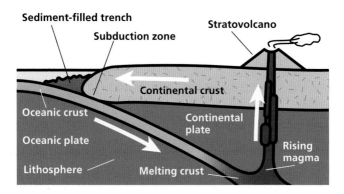

This creates rising streams of magma that accumulate within continental plates, forming chains of volcanoes.

All of these different types of tectonic events have contributed to the formation of Washington and Oregon.

Building Washington and Oregon

For hundreds of millions of years, the North American Plate crawled westward over the Pacific Plate at a rate of only a few millimeters a year. But this wasn't an uneventful period; like a plow, the eastbound Pacific Plate pushed enormous land-masses, called microcontinents, toward the North American Plate. These microcontinents were large islands in the early Pacific Ocean, much like New Zealand today, and the first one to slam into this portion of the North American plate is known as the Okanogan Microcontinent. When the Okanogan Microcontinent "docked" with the North American plate only 100 million years ago, it compressed the coastal plain accumulating on North America's shores and added a large amount of territory to what would become Washington State.

Around 50 million years after the Okanogan Microcontinent crashed into Washington, another huge landmass, called the Cascade Microcontinent, followed suit and smashed into Washington as well. But the Cascade Microcontinent was different—it already contained a chain of erupting volcanoes, and after the microcontinent docked with Washington, the volcanoes continued to spew lava. Approximately 10 million years later, the continued subduction of the Pacific Plate caused a chain of volcanoes to begin erupting in modern day Oregon and southern Washington. As lava and ash burst from the earth and began to accumulate, much of central Oregon was built up. The resulting volcanoes and mountains fell in line with the volcanoes of the newly docked Cascade Microcontinent, forming part of the Cascade Mountain Range we know today.

The final event that shaped modern day Washington and Oregon was the upthrust of sedimentary rocks on the states' western coasts. The sediment that collects in a subduction trench is too light to sink into the earth, so it continues to collect and build up. Eventually, so much sediment accumulates that it forms sedimentary rocks that are continuously pushed upwards by the further collection of sediment at the base of the subduction zone. This formed Oregon's Costal Range, Washington's enormous Olympic Mountains, and completed the shapes of each state as we know them today.

The Cascade Mountains and the Columbia Plateau

When the Cascade Microcontinent and Oregon's volcanic activity created a long chain of volcanoes, they formed the basis of the Cascade Mountain Range. But much more occurred between then and now to make the Cascade Mountains as large and rugged as they are today. After the original Cascade Range volcanoes came to rest in their current positions, they stopped erupting. It is not completely understood why, but 20 million years ago the volcanic activity moved from beneath the volcanoes to central and eastern Washington and Oregon. Here, new eruptions took place that caused enormous amounts of basalt lava to ooze over the landscape; when this happens, geologists refer to it as flood basalt. Over 63,000 square miles of basalt formed, covering all of southeastern Washington and nearly the entire eastern half of Oregon. This huge, relatively flat region is known today as the Columbia Plateau. Then, just 12 million years ago, the volcanic activity moved again, back to the Cascade Range, but it didn't reignite the old volcanoes. Instead, it began a new chain of volcanoes just east of the old ones. The original, older volcanoes and mountains are known today as the West Cascades and the newer, taller, more rugged peaks and active volcanoes are called the High Cascades. (Mount St. Helens is undoubtedly the most notorious of the High Cascades.) Aside from being perhaps the most prominent landmarks in Washington and Oregon, the High Cascades are a hotspot for rock hounds thanks to the unique geology and sky-high volcanic peaks, many of which are home to glaciers and year-round snow pack.

Precautions and Preparations

It may be surprising, but rock and mineral collecting often brings with it several dangers and legal concerns. It is always your responsibility to know where you can legally collect, which minerals may be hazardous to your health, and what you need to take with you in order to be prepared for any difficulties you may face. Here we will detail some of these issues.

Protected and Private Land

Both Washington and Oregon have many nationally protected parks, monuments and forests, as well as Native American reservations, all of which are areas where it is illegal to collect anything. In the dozens of state parks in each state, the rules can vary, so it is your responsibility to know if it is legal to collect rocks and minerals where you are. Collecting on federally owned land that is governed by the Bureau of Land Management is legal in both states, but only if you are collecting small amounts of material and are not going to sell what you've collected. Large fines await those caught collecting in protected areas. We encourage collectors to obey the law and leave the natural spaces wild and untouched for generations to come. It is always your responsibility to know whether or not the area in which you are collecting is protected.

As in any state, many places in Washington and Oregon are privately owned, including areas of coastline and large ranches that may not have obvious signage. Needless to say, you are trespassing if you collect on private property and the penalty may be worse than just a fine. In addition, property lines change frequently, as do property owners, so just because a landowner gave you permission to collect on their property last year doesn't mean the new owner will like you on their property this year. Finally, collectors also need to be careful not to cross onto a mining claim. Claims are plots of land where someone has paid for exclusive rights to mine and collect minerals, and no one else is allowed to do so there. Claims are required to be clearly marked and posted, however, so they should be obvious to collectors. In short, always be aware of where you are.

Though it's very unlikely, it is possible that you could encounter an unrestricted opening to one of the region's countless old mines. Due to the obvious dangers of such a place, you should never enter one, no matter how tempting it may be. Age and disrepair make collapse and poisonous gases a serious concern.

Dangerous Heights, Heat and Water

Rock collecting is not always the easygoing hobby that it initially seems to be. Adventurous rock hounds often find themselves in a number of dangerous places. In Washington and Oregon, where the soaring peaks and volcanoes of the Cascade Mountain Range are so prominent, falling from a great height or being hit by rolling boulders is a real possibility. We remind you never to take foolish risks or attempt any activity above your skill level, such as rock climbing, and never venture out alone. In the spring and fall, heavy rainfall can also cause mudslides to occur on slopes, making hiking and driving quite hazardous. On the dry eastern side of each state, summer temperatures can reach extreme highs, making heat exhaustion and sunburn serious concerns for rock hounds, so be sure to cover your skin and drink ample water.

Aside from the obvious dangers of heights and heat, coastal areas experience significant tides. Residents of the Pacific Northwest will be very familiar with them, but visitors may be surprised by the incredible tidal movements the coastlines of Washington and Oregon endure each day. When you're collecting on the shore, be sure to be familiar with the tidal forecast. Thankfully, tide charts that estimate and plot the high and low tides in a given area are widely available online, and you should obtain them before venturing on a shoreline collecting trip. If you don't, you may regret your decision; a fast-moving high tide can bring well over fifteen feet of water with it, which can wash away equipment left on the beach, sink your vehicle, and, worst of all, put you at risk of being stranded or even washed out to sea.

Sadly, some of the region's rivers, particularly those in eastern Washington, contain pollutants, such as arsenic, that concentrate in sediments. Public access areas at most of these rivers display signs warning of the dangers. Please heed these warnings and don't come into contact with water or riverbanks at these sites.

Effects of High Elevations

Washington and Oregon are home to stunning mountain passes and snowy volcano peaks, but with such high elevation areas, rock hounds from low-lying regions must be aware that they may become dizzy or short of breath when exerting themselves at altitude. The thin air can also cause you to tire quickly, so when on a mountainside, you'd do well to be extra careful, work slowly, and take plenty of breaks.

Equipment and Supplies

When you set out to collect rocks and minerals, there are a few items you don't want to forget. No matter where you are collecting, leather gloves are a good idea, as are knee pads if you plan to spend a lot of time on the ground. If you think you'll be breaking rock, bring your rock hammer (not a nail hammer) and eye protection. If the weather is hot and sunny, take the proper precautions and use sunblock, and bring sunglasses, a hat and ample water, both for drinking and for rinsing specimens. Lastly, bringing a global positioning system (GPS) device is a great way to prevent getting lost.

Collecting Etiquette

When collecting, be courteous; don't dig indiscriminately and don't take more than you need. Too often sites are closed to rock hounds because of the actions of careless or greedy collectors. To ensure great collecting sites for future rock hounds, dig carefully, take only a few specimens, and leave the location cleaner than you found it.

Potentially Dangerous Minerals

 The vast majority of minerals in Washington and Oregon are completely safe to handle, collect and store, but a few do have some inherent dangers associated with them. Potentially hazardous minerals included in this book are identified with the symbol shown above and more information about the minerals is detailed in the "notes" section on the pages listed below. Always follow our advice and take proper precautions when handling these minerals; see the pages listed below for specific advice.

Amphibole group (page 67)—rare varieties are asbestos; asbestiform minerals form as delicate, flexible fiber-like crystals that can easily become airborne and inhaled, posing a cancer risk

Arsenopyrite (page 77)—contains arsenic, a toxin

Boulangerite (page 257)—contains lead, a toxin

Cinnabar (page 101)—contains mercury, a toxin

Galena (page 263)—contains lead, a toxin

Mansfieldite (page 285)—contains arsenic, a toxin

Palygorskite (page 265)—asbestos mineral

Realgar (page 215)—contains arsenic, a toxin

Serpentine group (page 225)—rare varieties are asbestos

Stibnite (page 235)—contains antimony, a toxin

☢ Radioactive Minerals

In both Washington and Oregon, a few minerals can be found that contain uranium, a radioactive element. Radioactive materials can be very dangerous because they emit ionizing radiation, an invisible energy that emanates in all directions from its source and is able to penetrate solid objects. In animals, radiation affects cell structure, causing cells to mutate and leading to cancer. Luckily, most radioactive minerals emit relatively weak radiation and you would have to be in contact with them for extended amounts of time in order to cause even minor harm. In addition, the radioactive minerals in Washington and Oregon are quite rare and you won't likely come into contact with them unless you're specifically looking for them. But because of their beauty and interest, many radioactive minerals are still sought after by collectors, some of whom are not prepared for the dangers and great care necessary when collecting and storing radioactive minerals. Make no mistake; radioactivity is no laughing matter, and great harm can come to those who collect irresponsibly.

Only two radioactive minerals are covered in this book—autunite and meta-autunite on page 255—but other rare examples are present in the region as well.

Information for Radioactive Mineral Collectors

It is not recommended that amateurs collect any radioactive minerals. In fact, nobody should plan on starting a collection of radioactive minerals until they are fully prepared and have sufficient knowledge and a safe place to store specimens. If and when you feel you are ready, carefully read, understand, and follow this advice:

- **Obtain a Geiger counter**: The first essential piece of equipment you need is a Geiger counter. This device detects radioactivity and can tell you if a specimen is radioactive and how strongly so. While a properly calibrated Geiger counter can cost several hundred dollars, having one is absolutely crucial to the safe collecting and storage of radioactive minerals. When holding a Geiger counter near a radioactive specimen, an audible tone will sound and a needle will move along a scale to let you know how radioactive a specimen is. The higher the reading, the more dangerous the specimen.

- **Collect only low-radiation specimens**: U.S. Geiger counters typically measure radiation in units called millirems per hour, which is shortened to "mR/hr" or "mrem/hr." This signifies the amount of radiation your body would absorb during one hour in contact with a radioactive substance. A millirem is a rather small amount of radiation and our bodies receive at least one millirem of radiation per day from natural sources. Mineral specimens that emit between 0.1 and 20 mR/hr are relatively safe to collect and store.

- **Limit your exposure**: The maximum safe yearly dose of radiation is 500 millirems. Your body can sufficiently repair itself and eliminate this amount of radiation when absorbed over the course of a year.

Amounts of radiation in excess of 5,000 millirems a year can result in radiation sickness, cancer and even death. Most rock hounds won't be collecting radioactive minerals themselves, but some may purchase radioactive specimens from a shop. As a rule, obtain only small specimens, as they will contain less radioactive material, and interact with them as little as possible.

- **Consider safe storage before collecting**: Inexperienced collectors often don't realize that radioactive materials give off harmful gas as a result of radioactive decay (the natural process by which radioactive elements lose energy). In addition to the obvious threat of radiation, which can be thought of as an invisible poison, this gas is just one more reason why the safe storage of radioactive minerals is critical to consider before collecting. Since radiation from a small specimen will naturally die out within a few feet from the specimen (you can check the safe distance from your specimens with a Geiger counter), storing radioactive minerals in a garage, shed or other ventilated area far from people, pets and food storage is ideal. You may also want to consider purchasing a lead-lined container; lead is dense enough to shield you from all but the most powerful radioactive energy.

- **Use proper equipment**: When collecting and handling radioactive specimens, always wear gloves and a respirator. Most radiation will still be able to penetrate this equipment, but they will keep your skin and lungs out of direct contact with radioactive dust.

- **Inform yourself**: For more information and safety guidelines, visit the United States Nuclear Regulatory Commission's website (www.nrc.gov) or the Environmental Protection Agency's website (www.epa.gov).

Protected Fossils of Washington and Oregon

Fossils are the remains of ancient plants and animals that have turned to rock. Fossils are extremely popular collectibles for rock hounds, but in most states, including Washington and Oregon, there are strict rules about what you can collect. Certain fossils are protected due to their possible scientific significance while others have limits imposed on the quantity that can be collected. Anyone found violating these rules will be fined. The following are fossil-collecting guidelines that you must follow:

- Fossils of vertebrate animals (animals with a backbone), including fish, reptiles and mammals, are illegal to collect in all circumstances due to their scientific importance. If you happen to find such a fossil, tampering with the specimen is prohibited, but you are encouraged to make note of the fossil's location and contact the Oregon/Washington Bureau of Land Management (BLM) by visiting their website (www.blm.gov/or/index.php) or by calling their phone number (503-808-6002). The BLM will dispatch a paleontologist to examine the specimen.

- Petrified wood, or fossilized wood, is a beautiful and interesting collectible highly desired by rock hounds. Because of its desirability, however, there are limits as to how much you can collect. In Washington and Oregon, private collectors may collect no more than 25 pounds per day and no more than 250 pounds may be collected in a year. A special permit and contract must be obtained from the Bureau of Land Management if you plan to collect more or to sell your finds.

Hardness and Streak

There are two important techniques everyone wishing to identify minerals should know: hardness and streak tests. All minerals will yield results in both tests, as will certain rocks, which makes these tests indispensable to collectors.

The measure of how resistant a mineral is to abrasion is called hardness. The most common hardness scale, called the Mohs Hardness Scale, ranges from 1 to 10, with 10 being the hardest. An example of a mineral with a hardness of 1 is talc; it is a chalky mineral that can easily be scratched by your fingernail. An example of a mineral with a hardness of 10 is diamond, which is the hardest naturally occurring substance on earth and will scratch every other mineral. Most minerals fall somewhere in the range of 2 to 7 on the Mohs Hardness Scale, so learning how to perform a hardness test (also known as a scratch test) is critical. Common tools used in a hardness test include your fingernail, a U.S. nickel, a piece of glass and a steel pocket knife. There are also hardness kits you can purchase that have a tool of each hardness.

To perform a scratch test, you simply scratch a mineral with a tool of a known hardness—for example, we know a steel knife has a hardness of about 5.5. If the mineral is not scratched, you will then move to a tool of greater hardness until the mineral is scratched. If a tool that is 6.5 in hardness scratches your specimen, but a 5.5 did not, you can conclude that your mineral is a 6 in hardness. Two tips to consider: As you will be putting a scratch on the specimen, perform the test on the back side of the piece (or, better yet, on a lower-quality specimen of the same mineral), and start with tools softer in hardness and work your way up. On page 22, you'll find a chart that shows which tools will scratch a mineral of a particular hardness.

The second test every amateur geologist and rock collector should know is streak. When a mineral is crushed or powdered, it will have a distinct color—this color is the same as the streak color. When a mineral is rubbed along a streak plate, it will leave behind a powdery stripe of color, called the streak. This is an important test to perform because sometimes the streak color will differ greatly from the mineral itself. Hematite, for example, is a dark, metallic and gray mineral, yet its streak is a rusty red color. Streak plates are sold in some rock and mineral shops, but if you cannot find one, a simple unglazed piece of porcelain from a hardware store will work. There are only two things you need to remember about streak tests: If the mineral is harder than the streak plate, it will not produce a streak and will instead scratch the plate itself. Secondly, don't bother testing rocks for streak; they are made up of many different minerals and won't produce a consistent color.

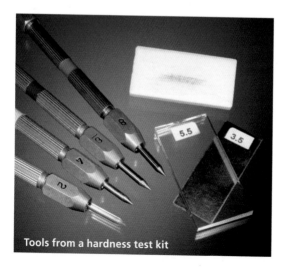

Tools from a hardness test kit

The Mohs Hardness Scale

The Mohs Hardness Scale is the primary measure of mineral hardness. This scale ranges from 1 to 10, from softest to hardest. Ten minerals commonly associated with the scale are listed here, as well as some common tools used to determine a mineral's hardness. If a mineral is scratched by a tool of a known hardness, then you know it is softer than that tool.

HARDNESS	EXAMPLE MINERAL	TOOL
1	Talc	
2	Gypsum	
2.5		Fingernail
3	Calcite	
3.5		U.S. nickel, brass
4	Fluorite	
5	Apatite	
5.5		Glass, Steel Knife
6	Orthoclase feldspar	
6.5		Streak Plate
7	Quartz	
7.5		Hardened steel file
8	Topaz	
9	Corundum	
9.5		Silicon carbide
10	Diamond	

For example, if a mineral is scratched by a U.S. nickel but not your fingernail, you can conclude that its hardness is 3, equal to that of calcite. If a mineral is harder than 6.5, or the hardness of a streak plate, it will have no streak and will instead scratch the streak plate itself, unless the specimen has weathered to a softer state.

Quick Identification Guide

Use this quick identification guide to help you determine which rock or mineral you may have found. Organized by color, this guide discusses some of the basic characteristics of the respective rocks and minerals, as well as the page number where you can read more. While the most common traits for each rock or mineral are listed here, be aware that your specimen may differ greatly.

<table>
<tr><th colspan="2">If white or colorless and...</th><th>then try...</th></tr>
<tr><td></td><td>Glassy ball-like crystals with many crystal faces growing within cavities in basalt</td><td>analcime, page 69</td></tr>
<tr><td></td><td>Glassy crystals with sharp points and a square cross section within cavities in basalt</td><td>apophyllite-(KF), page 73</td></tr>
<tr><td></td><td>Coarse, glassy needle-like crystals with striated (grooved) sides and angular tips</td><td>aragonite, page 75</td></tr>
<tr><td></td><td>Abundant, soft, blocky masses or steeply pointed six-sided crystals within cavities in rock</td><td>calcite, page 85</td></tr>
<tr><td></td><td>Glassy, blocky crystals that resemble leaning cubes and are found within cavities in basalt</td><td>chabazite-(Ca), page 89</td></tr>
<tr><td></td><td>Tiny ball-like masses, often intergrown with each other, found very rarely within cavities in basalt</td><td>cowlesite, page 109</td></tr>
<tr><td></td><td>Rare, tiny needle-like crystals arranged into ball-like masses or delicate "sprays" within cavities in basalt</td><td>dachiardite, page 113</td></tr>
</table>

WHITE OR COLORLESS

Quick Identification Guide (continued)

WHITE OR COLORLESS

(continued) **If white or colorless and...**	**then try...**
Hard masses consisting of coarse crystals arranged into radial "sprays," often on top of quartz	datolite, page 115
Soft blocky, angular crystals with a pearly luster and slightly curved faces	dolomite group, page 117
Tiny, soft and flexible, fiber-like crystals arranged into "sprays" and found within cavities in basalt	erionite, page 121
Blocky, angular opaque crystals or dull light-colored masses within coarse-grained rocks, like granite	feldspar group, page 123
Tiny, glassy, striated (grooved) crystals found rarely within andesite	fluorapatite, page 125
Tiny hexagonal (six-sided) glassy crystals with flat or hollow tips within cavities in basalt	gmelinite-(Na), page 281
Small, rounded ball-like formations with grooved surfaces within cavities in basalt	gyrolite, page 283
Lustrous coffin-shaped, blocky crystals with curved faces within cavities in basalt and other rocks	heulandite-(Ca), page 147
Soft, crumbly and stubby opaque crystals with a flat angled tip	laumontite, page 161

WHITE OR COLORLESS

(continued)	**If white or colorless and...**	**then try...**
	Hexagonal (six-sided) very thin, flat, plate-like crystals within cavities in basalt	lévyne, page 163
	Very delicate, flexible, hair-like crystals grown in tangled masses within cavities in basalt	mesolite, page 175
	Soft, "fuzzy" ball-like formations of tiny needle-like crystals, often within cavities in basalt or geodes	mordenite, page 181
	Delicate, brittle and glassy needle-like crystals arranged into radial "sprays" within cavities in basalt	natrolite, page 185
	Glassy opaque masses with no particular crystal shape, found filling cavities in rock	opal, page 191
	Flexible mats of material that resemble fabric and consist of fiber-like crystals	palygorskite, page 265
	Tiny, glassy ball-like crystals that are angular and often grown in stacks, often within cavities in basalt	paulingite-(Ca), page 289
	Rare, tiny, glassy and blocky elongated crystals within cavities in basalt	phillipsite, page 197
	Hard masses of angular crystals with curved edges, sometimes with a greenish tint	prehnite, page 201

Quick Identification Guide (continued)

WHITE OR COLORLESS

(continued)	**If white or colorless and...**	**then try...**
	Common light-colored masses, pebbles or six-sided pointed crystals that are very hard	quartz, page 209
	Coarse, soft and elongated needle-like crystals with a square cross section found within cavities in basalt	scolecite, page 223
	Lustrous crusts of intergrown crystals, found only in hot springs in central Oregon	stellerite, page 293
	Clusters of pearly crystals arranged into "wheat-sheaf" shapes and found within cavities in basalt	stilbite-(Ca), page 237
	Delicate, thin, blade-like crystals arranged into radial "sprays," often as a crust lining a cavity in basalt	thomsonite-(Ca), page 241
	Fibrous, silky masses containing elongated crystals, typically heavily intergrown with each other	tremolite, page 45
	Extremely rare tiny crystals with steep, sharp points found within vesicles in basalt	tschernichite, page 297
	Very rare hexagonal (six-sided), glassy crystals found within granite only in northern Washington	zektzerite, page 271

Quick Identification Guide (continued)

GRAY

If gray and...	then try...
Dense rock consisting of a fine-grained dark material containing embedded larger, lighter crystals	andesite, page 71
Blocky, wedge-shaped crystals that feel very heavy for their size	barite, page 81
Abundant dark rock with a very fine grain size, often containing many round bubble-like cavities	basalt, page 83
Very hard, translucent material that can't be scratched with a knife, often found on beaches	chalcedony, page 91
Dense, very hard, opaque rock that can't be scratched with a knife, often found on beaches	chert, page 95
Uncommon dark, coarse-grained rock containing many glassy black crystals	gabbro or diabase, page 131
Soft rock that fizzes in vinegar and is easily scratched by a knife	limestone, page 165
Glassy crusts within tuff found only in Oregon	mansfieldite, page 285
Shiny, nearly metallic, flexible and soft crystals or masses within rock	mica group, page 177

Quick Identification Guide (continued

	If gray and...	then try...
	Very fine-grained rock with even coloration that can be scratched with a knife	mudstone or siltstone, page 183
	Very hard rock that resembles quartz but has a grainy texture, often found on beaches	quartzite, page 213
	Light-colored, fairly hard rock abundant in the Cascade Mountains, often containing many gas bubbles	rhyolite, page 219
	Rocks consisting of many thin, flat, parallel layers that can often be separated with a knife	shale or slate, page 227
	Lumpy, lobed masses consisting of a chalky, soft exterior and a very hard interior found in southern Oregon	snakeskin "agate," page 291
	Very soft masses of flaky crystals with a very "slippery" feel	talc or soapstone, page 239
	Grainy, dense rock that can be scratched with a knife, often containing fragments of volcanic glass	tuff, page 245

GRAY

Quick Identification Guide (continued)

If black and...	then try...
Abundant silky, blocky crystals embedded in rock, especially granite	amphibole group, page 67
Hard blocky crystals embedded in dark rocks like gabbro, or found loose	augite, page 79
Dusty coatings or veins within rocks and minerals that often darken your hands	manganese oxides, page 173
Dense, hard material that resembles black glass	obsidian, page 187
Dark and glassy, blocky crystals within rocks, particularly dark rocks like gabbro	pyroxene group, page 205
Rare angular crystals or masses that may appear reddish in bright light, often grown alongside chalcopyrite	sphalerite, page 267
Radial ball-like growths of shiny material embedded within quartz, found in northwestern Washington	stilpnomelane, page 269

Quick Identification Guide (continued)

	If blue and...	then try...
BLUE	Very rare ball-like formations found alongside analcime in eastern Oregon	cavansite, page 277
	Soft, crumbly masses with no particular shape, often alongside malachite	chrysocolla, page 99
	Glass-like masses with no particular shape found filling cavities in rock	opal, page 191
	Very dark, almost black, hexagonal (six-sided) plate-like crystals within cavities in rhyolite in western Oregon	osumilite, page 287

	If yellow and...	then try...
YELLOW	Thin, flat and square plate-like radioactive crystals	autunite, page 255
	Common thin coatings or veins with no crystals on or in rocks	limonite, page 167
	Hard greenish masses within dark rocks like gabbro or found loose in sand	olivine group, page 189
	Hard, transparent, blocky masses found within basalt in southern Oregon	sunstone, page 295

Quick Identification Guide (continued)

GREEN

If green and...	then try...
Hard, striated (grooved) translucent crystals, often embedded in talc	actinolite, page 45
Soft, crumbly bluish masses or crusts found within cavities in basalt	celadonite, page 87
Soft, dark, "greasy" crusts or masses within cavities in basalt and other rocks	chlorite group, page 97
Very hard pea-green elongated crystals with striated (grooved) sides	epidote, page 119
Rare glassy masses exhibiting angular, blocky surfaces and internal cracks	fluorite, page 261
Very hard glassy crystals resembling faceted balls, often embedded within quartz or schist	garnet group, page 133
Rare, vividly colored, fairly soft material exhibiting no particular crystal shape, found only in southeastern Oregon	garnierite, page 279
Masses of dense translucent material found primarily on beaches	jade, page 151
Vividly colored botryoidal (grape-like) crusts or masses, or rare delicate needle-like crystals	malachite, page 171

	(continued) **If green and...**	**then try...**
	Hard glassy masses within rocks, particularly dark rocks like gabbro	olivine group, page 189
	Soft masses of dark material that feel "greasy" to the touch, often with a weathered brown exterior	serpentine group, page 225
	Rare dark needle-like crystals arranged into "sprays," often growing on quartz	tourmaline group, page 243

GREEN

	If brown and...	**then try...**
	Crusts of very hard material exhibiting rough, irregularly curving ridges and grooves	"angel wing" agate, page 49
	Blocky, angular crystals that feel very heavy for their size	barite, page 81
	Dense, very hard material unable to be scratched with a knife, often found on beaches	chalcedony, page 91
	Dense, very hard, opaque rock that can't be scratched with a knife, often found on beaches	chert, page 95
	Very soft, chalky masses or crusts that often exhibit cracking and swell when wet	clay minerals, page 103

BROWN

(continued) **If brown and...**	**then try...**
Very hard stubby crystals with a blocky shape, found only in Washington in skarn	clinozoisite, page 259
Soft blocky, angular crystals with a pearly luster and slightly curved faces	dolomite, page 117
Blocky, angular opaque crystals or dull light-colored masses within coarse-grained rocks like granite	feldspar group, page 123
Rocks containing material that resembles living creatures or shells	fossils, animal, page 127
Rocks containing material that resembles plants	fossils, plant, page 129
Very hard glassy crystals resembling faceted balls, often embedded within quartz or schist	garnet group, page 133
Dusty or metallic crusts with a rusty color that have a similarly colored streak	goethite, page 139
Very hard, opaque masses with a rough texture when fresh, but a smooth, waxy texture when weathered	jasper, page 153
Dusty, earthy rust-colored masses or coatings that often leave your hands brown after handling	limonite, page 167

BROWN

Quick Identification Guide (continued)

(continued)	**If brown and...**	**then try...**
	Very fine-grained rock with even coloration that can be scratched with a knife	mudstone or siltstone, page 183
	Very hard rock that resembles quartz but has a grainy texture, often found on beaches	quartzite, page 213
	Rough, crumbly rock composed of tiny grains of sand stuck together	sandstone, page 221
	Soft fine-grained rock consisting of many thin, flat, parallel layers than can be separated with a knife	shale, page 227
	Soft, light-colored blocky or blade-like crystals often found in sedimentary areas	siderite, page 231
	Very soft masses of flaky crystals with a very "slippery" feel	talc, page 239
	Grainy, dense rock that can be scratched with a knife, often containing fragments of volcanic glass	tuff, page 245
	Oddly rounded rocks, often with "fins" or other aerodynamic shapes	volcanic bombs, page 247
	Very hard, tiny rectangular crystals with pyramid-shaped tips and a square cross section	zircon, page 251

Quick Identification Guide (continued)

RED

If red and...	then try...
Grainy crusts of veins of red dust-like material	cinnabar, page 101
Very hard glassy crystals resembling faceted balls, often embedded within quartz or schist	garnet group, page 133
Very hard, opaque masses that cannot be scratched with a knife, often found on beaches	jasper, page 153
Glass-like masses with no particular shape found filling cavities in rock	opal, page 191
Vividly colored glassy crystals, often with an elongated rectangular shape	realgar, page 215

ORANGE

If orange and...	then try...
Vividly colored and very hard translucent masses containing concentric banding	agate, carnelian, page 51
Glassy, blocky crystals with flat faces, often found within thunder egg geodes	clinoptilolite, page 105
Delicate hair-like crystals arranged into tufts, often found within cavities in basalt	erionite, page 121

Quick Identification Guide (continued)

(continued) **If orange and...**	**then try...**
Clusters of pearly crystals arranged into "wheat-sheaf" shapes and found within cavities in basalt	stilbite-(Ca), page 237
Hard blocky masses containing copper-colored material within, found in basalt in southern Oregon	sunstone, page 295

If violet or pink and...	**then try...**
Very hard translucent masses containing concentric banding	agate, color variations, page 53
Hexagonal (six-sided) pointed crystals that are very hard	quartz, varieties, page 211
Hard glassy masses, typically crosscut with black veins of material	rhodonite, page 217
Very hard veins or masses of material, often embedded within other rocks or minerals	thulite, page 119

Quick Identification Guide (continued)

METALLIC

If metallic and...	then try...
Silvery diamond-shaped crystals or masses embedded in galena or quartz	arsenopyrite, page 77
Very rare magnetic masses with a brown surface coating, only found in southwestern Oregon	awaruite, page 275
Soft masses consisting of needle-like crystals that blacken your hands	boulangerite, page 257
Soft, brightly lustrous, brassy yellow mineral that often develops an orange or bluish tarnish	chalcopyrite, page 93
Very rare embedded brassy masses that are magnetic	cubanite, page 111
Dense, grainy masses with blocky surfaces that are very heavy for their size	galena, page 263
Very soft, malleable, brightly lustrous yellow metal, most often found in rivers	gold, page 141
Common dark metallic masses or plate-like crystals with a reddish streak	hematite, page 145
Tiny, thin hexagonal (six-sided) crystals or shiny grains in sand that are weakly magnetic	ilmenite, page 149

Quick Identification Guide (continued)

(continued) **If metallic and...** then try...

METALLIC

Black angular crystals or grains of sand that will bond strongly with a magnet — magnetite, page 169

Very soft, flexible, bluish gray, plate-like six-sided crystals or flaky masses — molybdenite, page 179

Brassy yellow cubic crystals, veins or masses, typically with grooved faces — pyrite, page 203

Brassy brown hexagonal (six-sided) crystals or masses that are magnetic — pyrrhotite, page 207

Soft, dark, elongated needle-like crystals embedded in quartz or rock — stibnite, page 235

If multicolored or banded and... then try...

MULTICOLORED OR BANDED

Very hard translucent masses containing ring-like banding within, often found on beaches — agate, page 47

Very hard translucent masses containing flat parallel layering that is unable to be scratched by a knife — agate, gravitationally banded, page 55

Very hard translucent masses containing moss-like tangles of colored material within — agate, moss, page 57

Quick Identification Guide (continued)

(continued) — vertical left margin: MULTICOLORED OR BANDED

(continued)	If multicolored or banded and...	then try...
	Very hard translucent masses containing feather- or smoke-like growths of material within	agate, plume, page 59
	Very hard translucent masses containing needles of other minerals within	agate, sagenitic, page 61
	Rough round masses of rock containing masses of chalcedony or agate within	agate, thunder eggs, page 63
	Very hard translucent masses containing round tube-like structures within	agate, tube, page 65
	Rock consisting of smaller rounded pebbles or rock fragments cemented together	conglomerate or breccia, page 107
	Round rocky masses with hollow centers, often lined with a crust of quartz or chalcedony	geodes, page 135
	Hard, dense rocks containing layers that often consist of different minerals	gneiss or schist, page 137
	Abundant, hard, mottled, coarse-grained rock consisting of many different minerals	granite, page 143
	Very hard, opaque masses that cannot be scratched with a knife, often found on beaches	jasper, page 153

Quick Identification Guide (continued)

(continued)	**If multicolored or banded and...**	**then try...**
	Very hard, colorful opaque masses that cannot be scratched with a knife, often found in desert regions	jasper, fancy, page 155
	Very hard, opaque masses that cannot be scratched with a knife and contain layers that resemble a landscape	jasper, picture, page 159
	Rocky masses that exhibit the traits of wood, including grain and growth rings	petrified wood, page 193
	Fine-grained rocks containing larger embedded crystals that are often elongated in shape	porphyry, page 199
	Soft, smooth, striped fragments found abundantly on beaches	shells, page 229
	Coarse-grained rock containing many well-developed crystals and strong variations in color	skarn, page 233
	Mottled, coarse-grained rocks abundant along the Cascade Mountain Range	volcanic rocks, page 249

Chabazite-(Ca) crystal groupings

Crystal-lined vesicle

Intergrown crystals

Rhombohedral crystals

Rhombohedral chabazite-(Ca) crystals

Sample Page

HARDNESS: 7 **STREAK:** White

Primary occurrence map

ENVIRONMENT: A generalized indication of the types of places where this rock or mineral can commonly be found. For the purposes of this book, the primary environments listed include shorelines (both ocean and inland lake), rivers (including riverbeds and banks), quarries, road cuts, mountains and fields (which can include any low-lying grasslands, ranches or deserts).

WHAT TO LOOK FOR: Common and characteristic identifying traits of the rock or mineral.

SIZE: The general size range of the rock or mineral. The listed sizes apply more to minerals and their crystals than to rocks, which typically form in masses or chunks.

COLOR: The colors the rock or mineral commonly exhibits.

OCCURRENCE: The difficulty of finding this rock or mineral. "Very common" means the material takes almost no effort to find if you're in the right environment. "Common" means the material can be found with little effort. "Uncommon" means the material may take a good deal of hunting to find, and most minerals fall in this category. "Rare" means the material will take great lengths of research, time and energy to find, and "very rare" means the material is so uncommon that you will be lucky to find even a trace of it.

NOTES: These are additional notes about the rock or mineral, including how to find it, how to identify it, how to distinguish it from similar minerals, and interesting facts about it.

WHERE TO LOOK: Here you'll find specific regions or towns where you should begin your search for the rock or mineral.

Actinolite crystals (green) in talc (tan)

Actinolite crystal mass

Actinolite in schist

Fibrous, silky beach-worn mass of tremolite

Actinolite-Tremolite series

HARDNESS: 5–6 **STREAK:** White

Occurrence

ENVIRONMENT: All environments

WHAT TO LOOK FOR: Elongated, striated (grooved), rectangular crystals embedded in rock or mica, or fibrous, silky masses

SIZE: Crystals of actinolite or tremolite are rarely more than an inch or two in length; masses can measure several inches

COLOR: Tremolite is white to gray, yellow to brown; actinolite is light to dark green, gray to black

OCCURRENCE: Uncommon

NOTES: In the chemical compositions of some minerals, an element can be replaced all or in part by another element without changing the mineral's structure. For example, during formation, some of the magnesium in tremolite can be exchanged for atoms of iron, which makes it actinolite. This close relationship is called a mineral series. Minerals in series can therefore be extremely difficult to distinguish from each other, though in the case of actinolite and tremolite, color is a pretty good distinguishing feature. Both minerals are members of the amphibole group (page 67), but tremolite is typically light colored while actinolite is often dark colored in shades of green. Both minerals form elongated, blocky crystals with striated (grooved) faces and are generally embedded in rock or other minerals, particularly talc (page 239). Some dark specimens may closely resemble tourmalines (page 243), but all tourmaline minerals are much harder. Other specimens appear as compact, fibrous masses, but perhaps the most famous form of this series is nephrite jade (page 151), a highly compact form of actinolite.

WHERE TO LOOK: Masses of tremolite can occasionally be found on the Washington and Oregon coasts, while fine crystals of actinolite are found in talc in Chelan County, Washington.

Rough, broken agate

Beach-worn agates

Pink coloration

Close-up of banding

Polished agates from San Juan Island, WA

Polished agate from Mount Rainier area, WA

Polished agate from western Oregon

Agate

HARDNESS: 7 **STREAK:** White

Occurrence

ENVIRONMENT: Shoreline, rivers, fields

WHAT TO LOOK FOR: Very hard, waxy, translucent, red, yellow or brown rounded masses of material displaying ring-like bands

SIZE: Agates range from pea-sized fragments to fist-sized masses

COLOR: Multicolored; color varies greatly, but banding is primarily yellow, red, brown, white or gray

OCCURRENCE: Uncommon

NOTES: Agates are a favored collectible among rock hounds in many states, but they are a mysterious one as well. These colorful gemstones formed in vesicles (gas bubbles) or other cavities within rocks, particularly basalt and rhyolite, and exhibit concentric ring-like banding much like the layers of an onion. They are composed of chalcedony (page 91), a microcrystalline variety of quartz (page 209), but it's not at all clear how agates got their characteristic bands. Geological mysteries notwithstanding, agates are very popular because, unlike most minerals, agates can be found lying on the surface of beaches, in rivers, and in gravel, making them easy to collect. Agates are found in this manner because they are so hard that weathering merely frees them from their host rock. Agates are identified by their hardness—a steel knife won't scratch them—and by their waxy surface texture, though they often resemble other varieties of microcrystalline quartz, such as jasper (page 153). Agates can be distinguished from such look-alikes by their translucency and concentric banding. Unbanded agate-like material is just chalcedony.

WHERE TO LOOK: In Washington, beaches on Camano and Whidbey Islands are well known for small agates, but beaches all along Oregon's coast are perhaps the best locations.

"Bubbly" botryoidal (grape-like) surfaces

Cross section

Surface detail

Irregular ridge-covered surface

Agate, "angel wing"

HARDNESS: 7 **STREAK:** White

Occurrence

ENVIRONMENT: Quarries, road cuts

WHAT TO LOOK FOR: Crusts of hard, waxy material that exhibit lumpy ridges or botryoidal (grape-like) surface textures

SIZE: Angel wing agates can be palm-sized and larger

COLOR: White to gray, yellow to brown; often multicolored

OCCURRENCE: Rare

NOTES: When it comes to unique formations of chalcedony (page 91), rock hounds have long had a habit of calling everything an "agate," whether it is banded or not. "Angel wing agates" are an example of this and are rarely, if ever banded, but do share a lot of similarities with plume agates (page 59). Formed in crevasses and cavities in rock, angel wing agates develop when water rich in silica (quartz material) seeps into a cavity and coats existing mineral formations, often clay. As more silica enters the space, it builds upon itself, growing inward in lumpy, irregular, and often botryoidal (grape-like) shapes. Some are branching and feather-like, hence the collectors' name for these crusts of chalcedony. Identification is easy based on visual characteristics alone, but always check hardness as it is possible that other minerals may share a similar appearance. In addition, the cross section of angel wing agates often reveals the mineral inclusions upon which the chalcedony accumulated, and the best examples will reveal beautiful plume-like structures when cut or broken. Angel wing agates are often found in sedimentary rocks, such as limestone.

WHERE TO LOOK: The area around Graveyard Point in Malheur County in eastern Oregon is known for angel wing agates, but beware of private claims. In Washington, these agates can rarely be found in veins near Mount Vernon.

49

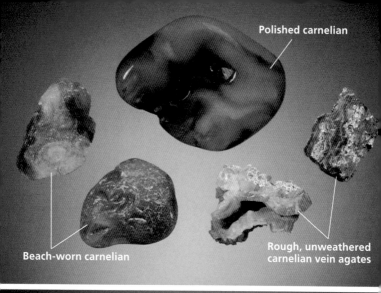

Polished carnelian

Beach-worn carnelian

Rough, unweathered carnelian vein agates

Carnelian agate

Agate, carnelian

HARDNESS: 7 **STREAK:** White

Occurrence

ENVIRONMENT: Shoreline, rivers, fields, mountains

WHAT TO LOOK FOR: Hard, waxy, translucent red, yellow or orange irregular masses of material, often displaying ring-like bands

SIZE: Agates range from pea-sized fragments to fist-sized masses

COLOR: Red to orange, yellow to brown

OCCURRENCE: Uncommon

NOTES: For hundreds of years, a variety of criteria have been used to categorize agate varieties. Agates have been classified according to everything from their structural features to superficial differences, like color. Carnelian agates, usually simply called carnelian, are an example of an agate variety identified by coloration and are known for their intense reds, oranges and yellow-browns. Often found along rivers and mountainsides, carnelian can form in vesicles (gas bubbles) within volcanic rocks (like most agates), or it can develop as veins within cracks and fissures in rocks. Like common agates, vesicular carnelian is often found in nodules (rounded masses) and is frequently rounded and smoothed by weathering. Vein carnelian takes more irregular shapes and is frequently less weathered and has very rough, ragged surfaces. In either case, a specimen of carnelian may or may not exhibit banding. Technically, unbanded specimens are merely chalcedony (page 91), but collectors generally don't distinguish banded from unbanded carnelian as long as a specimen has the characteristic coloration. Differentiating carnelian from other agates and chalcedony is as simple as noting its unusually vivid reddish orange color.

WHERE TO LOOK: Dozens of locations in Linn County, Oregon, produce carnelian, particularly in rivers. In Washington, various rivers in Lewis County are well known for carnelian.

51

Unpolished "holly blue" agates

Unpolished "Ellensburg blue" agate

Agate, color variations

HARDNESS: 7 **STREAK:** White

Occurrence

ENVIRONMENT: Shoreline, rivers, fields, road cuts

WHAT TO LOOK FOR: Hard, waxy masses or veins of colorful material containing concentric ring-like bands

SIZE: Can be found in a wide range of sizes, from pea-sized to softball-sized and rarely larger

COLOR: Multicolored; varies greatly, but primarily have different colored bands of yellow, brown, red, blue, purple or pink

OCCURRENCE: Rare

NOTES: Though agates form most often within vesicles (gas bubbles) in volcanic rocks, agates also form in other geological settings, including veins within cracks in other types of rock. These settings often include different mineral impurities, resulting in agates with unique and rare colorations. Several examples of these variations are found in the Pacific Northwest. "Holly blue agates," found near Sweet Home in western Oregon, are rare blue and purple agates that formed in vesicles and veins within rhyolite and are prized locally for their vivid coloration. Unfortunately, most of the area that once produced holly blue agates is now private. "Ellensburg blue agates," found near Ellensburg, Washington, are widely known for their delicate shades of blue and are often used by jewelers. Ellensburg blue agates are scarce, however, and even poor, unbanded specimens are highly sought after and valuable. The beautiful pink agates that occasionally turn up along Oregon's coast are more obtainable and sought after by tourists.

WHERE TO LOOK: The area around Sweet Home, Oregon, and Ellensburg, Washington, produce the rare blue and purple varieties, but beware of private land. Pink agates can be found along Oregon's Pacific Coast.

Gravitationally banded thunder egg agates

Parallel horizontal banding

Gravitational bands in a thunder egg agate

Agate, gravitationally banded

HARDNESS: 7 **STREAK:** White

Occurrence

ENVIRONMENT: Shoreline, rivers, fields

WHAT TO LOOK FOR: Very hard, waxy, translucent, red, yellow or brown rounded masses of material displaying parallel horizontal bands along the lower portion of the specimen

SIZE: Agates range from pea-sized fragments to fist-sized masses

COLOR: Multicolored; varies greatly, but primarily have different colored bands of yellow, red, brown, white or gray

OCCURRENCE: Common

NOTES: Second in abundance only to agates with the classic band-within-a-band pattern, gravitationally banded agates are a common and widespread variety of agate in Washington and Oregon. These unique agates exhibit a series of flat, horizontal parallel layers thought to have formed when an agate formed with an abnormal amount of water. This caused the silica (quartz material) that would normally form circular bands to sink and settle to the bottom of the cavity in which the agate formed. Also called "water-level agates" by collectors and known as "onyx" since antiquity, gravitationally banded agates are often found on beaches and riverbanks, as well as within the cores of thunder eggs (page 63), which formed within volcanic ash. The horizontal banding is contained within the agate, so a whole, unweathered agate won't offer any clues until cut or broken open. Once the horizontal bands are exposed, identification is no different than with other agates. Its appearance and high hardness should be more than enough to identify it.

WHERE TO LOOK: Gravitationally banded agates are found almost anywhere regular agates are, particularly on the Pacific Coast of both Washington and Oregon, and are common within thunder eggs, especially near Madras, Oregon.

Close-up of unpolished moss agate from Maury Mountain, Oregon

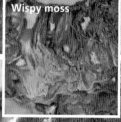

Wispy moss

Whole moss agate

Detail of polished moss agate

Agate, moss

HARDNESS: 7 **STREAK:** White

Occurrence

ENVIRONMENT: Shoreline, rivers, fields, road cuts

WHAT TO LOOK FOR: Very hard, waxy, translucent, red, yellow or brown rounded masses of material displaying tangled masses of moss-like or filamentous growths

SIZE: Agates range from pea-sized fragments to fist-sized masses

COLOR: Multicolored; varies greatly, but primarily have different colored bands of yellow, red, brown, white or gray

OCCURRENCE: Common

NOTES: Many agates contain inclusions, or growths of other minerals, embedded within them. Sometimes so many inclusions are present that it's hard to still consider the specimen an agate at all. This is the case with moss agates, which contain seemingly organic tangles of hair-like growths. When moss agates were first studied hundreds of years ago, it was believed that they actually contained fossilized moss. Today, we know that the moss-like growths are actually tiny channels created by a unique chemical reaction between tiny grains of metal-bearing minerals and silica (quartz material) in an agate that hasn't finished forming and is still soft. As the grains are altered by the silica, they form a hard shell that increases the pressure within the grain. The grain then bursts forth from its shell, only to meet with more silica, which forms another shell. This process continues, propelling the grain throughout the semi-soft agate, leaving a colored trail behind it. As this happens with hundreds of other grains, the intertwining moss-like growths appear. Don't confuse moss agates with tube agates (page 65).

WHERE TO LOOK: Moss agates are quite widespread and can be found anywhere regular agates are found, particularly on the Pacific Coast and throughout the Cascade Range.

"Nyedigger plume" agate

Unpolished plume agate

Plume agate from Robinson Ranch, OR

"Regency rose" rare pink plume

Plume agate from Priday Ranch, OR

Plume agate from Stinkingwater, OR

Plume agate from Sheep Creek, OR

Plume agates from Graveyard Point, OR

"Carey Ranch plume"

"Robinson Ranch plume"

"Priday Ranch plume"

Agate, plume

HARDNESS: 7 **STREAK:** White

ENVIRONMENT: Rivers, fields, road cuts

Occurrence

WHAT TO LOOK FOR: Very hard, waxy, translucent, red, yellow or brown rounded masses; exterior surfaces are lumpy but internal formations are plant- or feather-like

SIZE: Plume agates can be found in veins more than a foot long

COLOR: Multicolored; varies greatly, but primarily white to gray, red to brown, yellow to orange

OCCURRENCE: Rare

NOTES: One of the most interesting aspects of collecting agates (page 47) is searching for specimens with inclusions, or formations of other minerals, within the agate. Plumes are one of the more fantastic examples of inclusions and appear as branching plant-like, smoke-like or feather-like formations. These beautiful, often whimsical growths are believed to form when iron- or manganese-bearing solutions slowly enter a body of chalcedony (page 91) while it is in a soft, gel-like state. As the particles of minerals move around within the gel, they adhere to each other randomly, eventually forming the distinctive plume shapes. Plume agates tend to form in veins, not vesicles (gas bubbles) like other agates, which means that they can grow to very large sizes. Externally, the agates often appear as irregular masses of chalcedony, often with jagged or botryoidal (grape-like) surfaces, and the plumes only show once the agates are cut or broken. Though these are always called plume agates, most are not banded and their value comes from the color and quality of the plume formations; pinks are highly prized.

WHERE TO LOOK: There are several locations along the Oregon-Idaho border, including some commercial mines, so be very wary of private property.

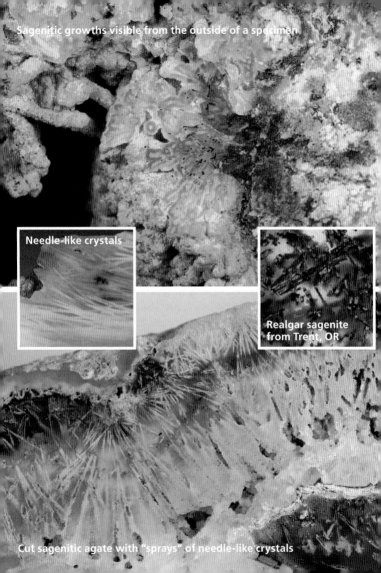

Sagenitic growths visible from the outside of a specimen

Needle-like crystals

Realgar sagenite from Trent, OR

Cut sagenitic agate with "sprays" of needle-like crystals

Agate, sagenitic

HARDNESS: 7 **STREAK:** White

Occurrence

ENVIRONMENT: Shoreline, rivers, fields, road cuts

WHAT TO LOOK FOR: Very hard, waxy, translucent, red, yellow or brown rounded masses of material containing needle-like crystals of other minerals within

SIZE: Agates range from pea-sized fragments to fist-sized masses

COLOR: Multicolored; varies greatly, but primarily have varying bands of yellow, red, brown, white or gray

OCCURRENCE: Uncommon

NOTES: Like plume agates (page 59), sagenitic agates are agates that contain inclusions, or growths of other minerals, embedded within the agate. Sagenitic agates contain "sagenite," which actually isn't a particular mineral and is instead a term used to describe any long, slender, needle-like mineral crystals that are embedded in quartz or chalcedony. This can include aragonite (page 75), realgar (page 215), zeolite minerals, such as natrolite (page 185), and many other minerals. Because many of these minerals often grow within the cavities and vesicles (gas bubbles) that also typically produce agates, specimens of sagenitic agates are not rare. In sagenitic agates, the needle-like crystals formed within the agate when it was still in a soft, semi-solid state, and many of the sagenite inclusions are arranged into fan-shaped clusters; this is particularly true for inclusions of zeolite minerals. And because these minerals are so much softer than the agate material that surrounds them, they are often eroded, forming pitted surfaces on the agate.

WHERE TO LOOK: Agates with sagenitic inclusions can be found in many of the same places as regular agates, particularly the beaches of the Pacific Coast. The area around Trent, Oregon, has produced rare and fine examples.

Whole thunder eggs from central Oregon

Desirable blue interior

Thunder egg geode

Gravitationally banded thunder egg agates

Agate, thunder eggs

HARDNESS: N/A **STREAK:** N/A

Occurrence

ENVIRONMENT: Fields, quarries, road cuts

WHAT TO LOOK FOR: Spherical, lumpy masses of rock containing hard, translucent, banded or layered material within

SIZE: Thunder eggs are rarely larger than a grapefruit

COLOR: Varies greatly; exterior white to gray or brown, interior white to gray, blue, tan to yellow, red to pink or orange

OCCURRENCE: Uncommon

NOTES: Thunder eggs are a particularly interesting variety of agate (page 47) that formed in a completely different geological environment than most other agates. Most agates formed within vesicles (gas bubbles) in recently cooled lava (molten rock), such as basalt (page 83). Thunder eggs formed within hollow pockets in tuff (page 245), a type of rock formed by the solidification of volcanic ash. These pockets were made by the rapid expansion of hot gases, leaving a void that later filled in with a solution bearing silica, the quartz material that forms all agates. As the silica crystallized and layered to form an agate, it also adhered to the surrounding tuff, forming a round shell of hard rock surrounding the agate core. Therefore, when thunder eggs are found, they appear only as round rocks. One might think that this would make them impossible to find, but in most localities, the tuff in which the thunder eggs formed has decayed to a soft, muddy clay and the hard thunder eggs are conspicuous. Finally, some thunder eggs are hollow, making them geodes (page 135).

WHERE TO LOOK: Pay-to-dig services are available throughout Oregon, particularly near Madras, where some of the finest specimens are found. In Washington, thunder eggs can be found buried in clay near Naches and Ellensburg.

Agate, tube

HARDNESS: 7 **STREAK:** White

Occurrence

ENVIRONMENT: Shoreline, rivers, fields, road cuts

WHAT TO LOOK FOR: Very hard, waxy, translucent, red, yellow or brown rounded masses of material displaying curving structures that appear hollow or tube-like

SIZE: Agates range from pea-sized fragments to fist-sized masses

COLOR: Multicolored; varies greatly, but primarily have different colored bands of yellow, red, brown, white or gray

OCCURRENCE: Uncommon

NOTES: Agates rarely form alone in a vesicle (gas bubble) or other cavity in rock. The other minerals growing in the same space may even be incorporated into the body of an agate as an inclusion. Tubes are one such inclusion and, as their name suggests, they appear as tiny hollow channels within an agate. Depending on the specimen, they can form in more than one way. In many, the tubes formed much in the same way as moss agates (page 57); tiny grains of metal-bearing minerals react chemically with the silica (quartz material) from which the agate is formed. Such tubes are often seen as tangles of curving structures in Oregon's thunder eggs (page 63). In addition, when minerals with long, slender, needle-like crystals, such as aragonite (page 75), are encased within an agate and weather away, they leave behind a slender channel. Sometimes these tubes remain hollow, but in others they are filled by quartz. It can be easy to confuse tube agates with moss agates, but the "moss" in moss agates tends to be much more plentiful.

WHERE TO LOOK: Many thunder eggs from the area around Madras, Oregon, contain tubes. Tube agates can also be found on the Pacific Coast of Washington and Oregon.

Large hornblende crystal

Arfvedsonite crystal

Arfvedsonite in feldspar

Hornblende in granite

Arfvedsonite in feldspar

Amphibole group

HARDNESS: 5–6 **STREAK:** White

Occurrence

ENVIRONMENT: All environments

WHAT TO LOOK FOR: Hard, dark-colored, blocky elongated crystals or black masses embedded within rock, particularly granite

SIZE: Most amphibole specimens are no larger than an inch

COLOR: Gray to black, dark green to yellow or brown

OCCURRENCE: Common; crystals are rare

NOTES: The amphiboles are a large group of minerals closely related to the pyroxenes (page 205). Rock-building minerals, amphiboles are found primarily as dark grains or masses and help form dozens of different rock types, particularly volcanic rocks like granite (page 143). Many amphiboles have a silky or fibrous appearance; when combined with their fairly high hardness, this can help collectors identify otherwise nondescript masses. But collectors want crystals, and of the many amphibole minerals present in both states—hornblende, arfvedsonite, anthophyllite, riebeckite, actinolite and tremolite, just to name a few—only a few are found as fine crystals. Hornblende, one of the world's most common minerals, can be found as lustrous black, blocky and angular crystals within various rocks. Similarly, arfvedsonite appears as elongated rectangular crystals commonly embedded within feldspars (page 123). Actinolite and tremolite (page 45) are fairly common and collectible, appearing as fibrous white or green masses. Many amphiboles are very similar, and additional research is often necessary to identify individual group members. Finally some rare examples are asbestos and consist of flexible hair-like fibers.

WHERE TO LOOK: Crystals of arfvedsonite are found at Washington Pass in Okanogan County, Washington, and tiny crystals of fluoro-edenite are found in Douglas County, Oregon.

Mass of intergrown crystals

Highly transparent coloration

Side view of crystal

Crystal cluster

Well-defined crystal shape

Two large intergrown crystals

Analcime

HARDNESS: 5–5.5 **STREAK:** White

Occurrence

ENVIRONMENT: Rivers, quarries, road cuts

WHAT TO LOOK FOR: Small light-colored crystals that are glassy and round and grow within vesicles (gas bubbles) in basalt

SIZE: Individual analcime crystals are typically smaller than a pea, but can occasionally grow up to an inch across

COLOR: Very commonly colorless to white; yellow to brown

OCCURRENCE: Uncommon

NOTES: Analcime is one of Washington and Oregon's numerous zeolites, the group of minerals that form in vesicles (gas bubbles) in basalt as it is affected by water. Analcime is popular because it is often found well crystallized, and while some zeolites are very difficult to identify, analcime is easy to identify due to its uniquely shaped trapezohedral crystals. These crystals have 24 faces and look like faceted balls. In addition, analcime is brightly lustrous and very commonly colorless; it's sometimes so clear and transparent that what lies behind a crystal is visible (though larger crystals are typically more opaque). These traits are so distinctive that any crystal matching this description within a vesicle can only be analcime. Sometimes a thin crust of many tiny intergrown analcime crystals can line all or part of a vesicle, and in this case analcime could be confused with phillipsite (page 197), which can form similar intergrowths. While analcime is slightly harder, magnification will be your best aid as phillipsite crystals are blockier and more rectangular. Finally, some garnets (page 133) form similar crystals, but all are harder and don't grow in vesicles.

WHERE TO LOOK: Basalt quarries and road cuts in Grant County, Oregon, are very lucrative, particularly near Ritter. In Washington, the areas around Kalama and Porter are well known.

Andesite

Embedded feldspar crystals (white)

Close-up of texture

Fine-grained andesite

Andesite

HARDNESS: 5–6 **STREAK:** N/A

Occurrence

ENVIRONMENT: Mountains, rivers, road cuts

WHAT TO LOOK FOR: Dark gray, dense rock containing highly visible light-colored grains and crystals embedded throughout

SIZE: Andesite can be found in any size

COLOR: Gray to dark gray with lighter colored spots throughout

OCCURRENCE: Common

NOTES: Like basalt (page 83) and rhyolite (page 219), andesite is an igneous rock produced when volcanoes erupt lava, or molten rock, onto the earth's surface. Named for the Andes Mountains of South America, where the rock was first studied, andesite is particularly common in the volcanic mountain ranges that encircle the Pacific Ocean. This is because the tectonic plate (page 8) that underlies the Pacific Ocean is being forced underneath the moving continents and deep into the earth's hot molten layer, called the mantle. There, it melts, creating a range of inland volcanoes that erupt the melted oceanic material onto the surface. Because ocean floors are made of basalt, we would expect the resulting eruptions to produce basalt as well, but andesite lava is unique. When still deep in the earth, the molten basalt was "contaminated" by other rock of differing composition, such as granite. As a result, andesite, found on many of Washington and Oregon's mountains, has a dark, dense and fine-grained basalt-like structure, but contains larger light-colored crystals of feldspar and mica. This is referred to as a porphyritic texture and is the primary means of distinguishing andesite from basalt and rhyolite.

WHERE TO LOOK: Andesite is present along much of the Cascade Range, but Mount Baker, near Bellingham, Washington, exhibits particularly beautiful columnar formations.

Apophyllite crystals

Sharp, well-formed crystal shapes

Mass of crystals

Flat-faced crystals

Phillipsite crystals

Basalt

Smaller surface crystals

Apophyllite-(KF)

HARDNESS: 4.5–5 **STREAK:** White

Occurrence

ENVIRONMENT: Rivers, quarries, road cuts

WHAT TO LOOK FOR: Small glassy crystals with a square cross section formed in vesicles (gas bubbles) in basalt

SIZE: Apophyllite-(KF) crystals are typically no larger than your thumbnail, but can rarely grow to an inch or more in size

COLOR: Colorless to white

OCCURRENCE: Rare in Washington; uncommon in Oregon

NOTES: There are several varieties of apophyllite around the world, but apophyllite-(KF), the potassium- and fluorine-bearing variety, is the most abundant and the only variety you're likely to find in Washington and Oregon. While not a member of the zeolite family of minerals, it is almost always found in vesicles (gas bubbles) in basalt alongside zeolites, such as stilbite-(Ca) (page 237) and natrolite (page 185). And, luckily for rock hounds, apophyllite-(KF) is typically found crystallized, which makes identification particularly easy. Apophyllite-(KF) crystals are normally short and often very square, almost cubic in shape. The colorless to white crystals will ideally taper to a point, but often end in flat surfaces. Apophyllite-(KF) also has perfect cleavage in one direction, which means that when carefully struck, a crystal will break to yield a perfectly flat surface that can sometimes resemble a crystal face. Apophyllite-(KF) is normally glassy and brightly lustrous, but not on a surface that has been cleaved. Instead, cleaved surfaces are pearly, often with a rainbow-like play of color.

WHERE TO LOOK: In Washington, the basalt formations near Bucoda are lucrative, as is the Kalama area. In Oregon, any zeolite-bearing basalts are promising, especially near Spray.

Intergrown needle-like crystals

Needle-like crystals

Aragonite on chalcedony

Aragonite crystal clusters coated with chalcedony

Aragonite

HARDNESS: 3.5–4 **STREAK:** White

Occurrence

ENVIRONMENT: Quarries, road cuts, mountains

WHAT TO LOOK FOR: Delicate, glassy, needle-like crystals with striated (grooved) sides, grown in often poorly organized groups

SIZE: Individual aragonite crystals are typically no longer than an inch while crystal groups can measure several inches

COLOR: Colorless to white, yellow to brown

OCCURRENCE: Uncommon

NOTES: Aragonite is a unique mineral: it has the same chemical composition as calcite (page 85), but it has a distinct crystal structure because it formed under different conditions. The primary difference is that aragonite's internal structure is more compact, making it harder than calcite and distinguishing it as a separate mineral. Its crystals also look different than calcite's; most of the time, aragonite crystals are long, slender colorless needles with striated (grooved) faces and a more-or-less square cross section. These beautiful crystals are primarily found as disorganized clusters atop chalcedony (page 91), quartz (page 209), or calcite and formed within cavities in basalt or other rocks. Nevertheless, it's easy to confuse aragonite's crystals with those of other minerals, particularly zeolites such as natrolite (page 185). Zeolites, however, are more abundant and won't fizz when placed in vinegar as aragonite eventually will. Like many minerals, aragonite can also form in white masses that are difficult to identify when no crystal structure is present, so you'll have to rely on its hardness and the vinegar test.

WHERE TO LOOK: The area around Kalama in Cowlitz County, Washington, produces beautiful crystal clusters, particularly within cavities in road cuts. In Oregon, locations in Lane County produce similar crystal clusters.

Arsenopyrite (silver-gray) intergrown with quartz (white)

Arsenopyrite (silvery) with galena (dark)

Crude crystal

Quartz (white)

Arsenopyrite (silver-gray)

⚠ **Arsenopyrite**

HARDNESS: 5.5–6 **STREAK:** Grayish black

Occurrence

ENVIRONMENT: Quarries, road cuts, mountains

WHAT TO LOOK FOR: Hard, metallic silver masses or diamond-shaped crystals, often embedded in rock alongside galena

SIZE: Masses of arsenopyrite typically measure less than a few inches in size, while crystals are often smaller than ⅛ inch

COLOR: Steel-gray to silver-white; sometimes has a brassy coating

OCCURRENCE: Rare

NOTES: As its name suggests, arsenopyrite contains arsenic, but as its arsenic content is chemically bonded to iron and sulfur, arsenopyrite is relatively safe to collect and handle (as long as you are careful not to inhale any dust created by the mineral). While similar in name, arsenopyrite is not actually related to pyrite (page 203), though the two minerals share many traits. Arsenopyrite is brightly metallic with a silver-gray color and is quite hard and brittle. Frequently occurring as masses embedded in rock or quartz, arsenopyrite is rarely found crystallized, but when it is, it forms as small wedge-like crystals with diamond-shaped cross sections. Massive arsenopyrite can exhibit a striated (grooved) or blocky structure when broken, which can aid in identification. Though a few other Washington and Oregon minerals may share a similar coloration, arseno-pyrite's hardness is distinctive in the region. Galena (page 263) can be very similar visually, but is much softer and feels much heavier than arsenopyrite. Silver, though rarely found in the region, is much softer and often has a dusty black surface coating.

WHERE TO LOOK: Dozens of old mines in Chelan County, Washington, produce massive arsenopyrite embedded in rock, as do those in Snohomish County. In Oregon, Baker and Josephine counties have yielded many specimens.

Loose augite crystals

Cross section

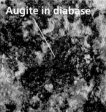

Augite in diabase

Augite masses in gabbro

Augite

HARDNESS: 5–6 **STREAK:** Greenish

Occurrence

ENVIRONMENT: Mountains, quarries, road cuts

WHAT TO LOOK FOR: Small, stout, glassy black crystals with angular faces, often embedded in dark rocks

SIZE: Augite specimens are rarely larger than a thumbnail, and crystals tend to be smaller than ½ inch in any dimension

COLOR: Black to greenish black, brown

OCCURRENCE: Common

NOTES: Augite is the most common member of the pyroxene mineral group (page 205), a large family of rock-builders that are primarily found as constituents of igneous and metamorphic rocks. The Pacific Northwest—Oregon, in particular—is fortunate to be home to some of the best specimens of augite in the country, some of which are perfectly crystallized and exemplify the mineral. Its crystals are short and barrel-like with many blocky, angular faces all around and a shallow point on each end. Many crystals are so stout that they are as wide as they are long. In addition, when viewed on-end or in cross section, well-formed crystals exhibit an octagonal (eight-sided) outline. Combined with their usual black to greenish coloration and glassy luster, fine crystals of augite are quite easy to identify. Nondescript black masses of augite embedded in rocks like gabbro and diabase are more difficult to identify. To do so, look for very square, blocky, step-like breaks. These are caused by augite's nearly 90 degree cleavage (its distinct breaking pattern).

WHERE TO LOOK: One of the most famous localities in the United States is the Cedar Butte area in Tillamook County, Oregon, where loose crystals can be found on roadside hills, eroded out of their host rock. In Washington, the Vesper Peak area in Snohomish County has produced crystals.

Large blocky crystal

Smaller intergrown crystals

Cross section

Crystal cluster

Steeply pointed crystal

Barite (Baryte)

HARDNESS: 3–3.5 **STREAK:** White

Occurrence

ENVIRONMENT: Mountains, road cuts, quarries

WHAT TO LOOK FOR: Light-colored blocky crystals that feel very heavy for their size and have a square- or diamond-shaped cross section, often with steep, wedge-like tips

SIZE: Individual crystals of barite can be as large as your palm, but most are thumbnail-sized or smaller

COLOR: Colorless to white or gray, yellow to brown, rarely bluish

OCCURRENCE: Uncommon

NOTES: Barite, spelled "baryte" everywhere but the United States, is the world's most abundant barium-bearing mineral, the element from which barite gets its name. Barium, used in fireworks and oil drilling, also lends barite one of its most diagnostic traits—the dense metallic element gives barite a relatively high specific gravity. This means that the density of barite is abnormally high for a non-metallic mineral, making even small specimens feel very heavy. Barite crystals can take several forms, but in Washington and Oregon, thick tabular (flat, plate-like) crystals with a square- or diamond-shaped cross section are common. Such crystals are frequently intergrown with each other. More rarely, blocky crystals of barite end with a steep, sharp, wedge-shaped point. Barite can also exhibit a third shape—very flat tabular crystals arranged into stacks that resemble the pages of a book. All of barite's crystal shapes are distinctive; when combined with its high density, differentiating it from look-alikes, such as calcite (page 85), is relatively easy.

WHERE TO LOOK: Many localities in King County, Washington, particularly those in mountainous areas, produce beautiful bladed crystals. In Oregon, the area around Lowell in Lane County produces some of the best specimens.

Basalt

Crystal-lined vesicles

Beach-worn basalt

Basalt porphyry

Scoria (light-weight basalt with many vesicles)

Rough weathered basalt

Iron-coated basalt

Basalt

HARDNESS: 5–6 **STREAK:** N/A

Occurrence

ENVIRONMENT: All environments

WHAT TO LOOK FOR: Dark, gray to black, dense, fine-grained rock, often containing many vesicles (gas bubbles)

SIZE: Can be found in any size, from pebbles to entire mountains

COLOR: Gray to black, often with a green or reddish brown tint

OCCURRENCE: Very common

NOTES: Basalt is one of the most prevalent volcanic rocks in Washington and Oregon; in fact, it underlies a huge amount of each state. It is a direct result of volcanic activity and formed when a vent in the earth's crust erupted lava, or molten rock, onto the earth's surface. Unlike molten rock deep within the earth that is insulated by the earth's hot interior and cools very slowly, lava on the earth's surface cools rapidly when exposed to the atmosphere. This causes it to harden so quickly that none of the minerals within it—mostly plagioclase feldspar, olivine and pyroxenes, as well as some amphiboles and magnetite—have enough time to crystallize to a large, visible size. The result is a dense, very fine-grained rock with an even-colored appearance. This rapid cooling process trapped gases in the lava, which formed vesicles (gas bubbles) where other minerals, particularly zeolites, could form later. Identification of basalt is fairly easy due to its abundance and dark coloration, though you may confuse it with andesite (page 71) or rhyolite (page 219). Andesite, however, often contains large light-colored grains while rhyolite is always much lighter colored overall.

WHERE TO LOOK: Basalt is very widespread. It is prevalent and easy to collect on the coastal shores of Washington, as well as in road cuts in the central and eastern areas of Oregon.

Calcite crystals

Calcite on thomsonite

Rhombohedral cleavage

Sharp calcite crystals

Calcite mass on schist

Beach-worn calcite in rock

Tiny intergrown crystals

Calcite

HARDNESS: 3 **STREAK:** White

Occurrence

ENVIRONMENT: All environments

WHAT TO LOOK FOR: Light-colored pointed crystals or blocky masses and veins that are easily scratched with a U.S. nickel

SIZE: Crystals can range from pinhead-sized to fist-sized and rarely larger; irregular masses can be any size

COLOR: Colorless to white; often yellow to brown when impure

OCCURRENCE: Very common

NOTES: Found virtually anywhere in Washington and Oregon in one form or another, calcite is one of the most common minerals on earth and is therefore one of the most important minerals for all collectors to be able to identify. Calcite consists of calcium carbonate and has numerous crystal forms; when well crystallized, it most often occurs as slender six-sided crystals that terminate with steep points, but crystals can also resemble blocky rhombohedrons (a shape resembling a leaning cube). As with any mineral, however, crystals are less common than white masses or veins within rock. In the Pacific Northwest, calcite commonly forms in vesicles (gas bubbles) in basalt alongside a number of other of minerals, many of which look like calcite. Look-alikes include quartz (page 209), apophyllite-(KF) (page 73), and zeolites, such as chabazite-(Ca) (page 89). Luckily, calcite is also easy to identify. First, calcite is softer than the previously mentioned minerals and a U.S. nickel will scratch it. Second, calcite effervesces (bubbles) in acid and even a small drop of vinegar will cause calcite to fizz and dissolve. Finally, when carefully broken, any specimen of calcite, even massive chunks, will cleave into perfect rhombohedrons.

WHERE TO LOOK: Found everywhere, but basalt quarries in Drain, Goble and Rainier, Oregon, are known for fine specimens.

Botryoidal celadonite mass in basalt vesicle

Celadonite in vesicle

Celadonite on quartz in vesicle

Large chalky masses of weathered celadonite

Celadonite

HARDNESS: 2 **STREAK:** Pale green

ENVIRONMENT: Road cuts, mountains, rivers, quarries Occurrence

WHAT TO LOOK FOR: Very soft, chalky, bluish green masses, most often within vesicles (gas bubbles) in basalt

SIZE: Individual crystals are microscopic, but crusts and masses can measure several inches

COLOR: Blue-green to green

OCCURRENCE: Common

NOTES: A member of the mica group of minerals (page 177), celadonite is a very colorful and common mineral in Washington and Oregon. However, despite its distinctive vivid blue-green coloration, it is not generally a highly sought-after collectible. That's because celadonite's crystals are microscopic. Unlike most mica minerals, which form as stacks of thin, flexible sheet-like crystals, celadonite's microcrystals tend to grow in compact masses that fill the cavity in which they grew. Since celadonite primarily forms within vesicles (gas bubbles) and other cavities in weathering volcanic rocks such as basalt, it is mostly found as embedded featureless green masses. Such specimens can be identified by celadonite's characteristic color and very low hardness—you can scratch it with your fingernails. In addition, celadonite easily weathers to a crumbly, chalky clay-like material, especially when freed from its host rock. Finer specimens do exist, however. Even though its crystals are too small to see, celadonite can form as interesting botryoidal (grape-like) or "fuzzy" masses in vesicles that are still partially hollow.

WHERE TO LOOK: Many places along the Clackamas River in Oregon produce masses of celadonite in basalt. In Washington, road cuts in Cowlitz County produce specimens.

Chabazite-(Ca) crystal groupings

Crystal-lined vesicle

Tiny intergrown crystals

Rhombohedral crystals

Rhombohedral chabazite-(Ca) crystals

Chabazite-(Ca)

HARDNESS: 4–5 **STREAK:** White

Occurrence

ENVIRONMENT: Rivers, quarries, road cuts

WHAT TO LOOK FOR: Light-colored rhombohedral crystals (shaped like a leaning cube) within vesicles (gas bubbles) in basalt

SIZE: Crystals are typically no larger than your thumbnail

COLOR: Colorless to white or cream-colored; when impure, commonly yellow to brown, pink, orange to red

OCCURRENCE: Uncommon

NOTES: Chabazite-(Ca) is one of Washington and Oregon's many zeolite minerals—the group of chemically complex minerals that form in vesicles (gas bubbles) in basalt as it is affected by mineral-bearing groundwater. Though several varieties of chabazite exist, the calcium-rich variety is the only one present in the region. Technically identified as the calcium-rich type by the "-(Ca)" after its name, it is typically just called chabazite. Chabazite-(Ca) is a particularly easy zeolite to identify. It forms as rhombohedral crystals, crystals that appear blocky and resemble a leaning or skewed cube. Two or more crystals are often found intergrown, or twinned, resulting in what appears to be a crystal with extra triangular points jutting from its faces. It can also form crusts of many tiny crystals that line the inside of a vesicle, and well-formed chabazite-(Ca) exhibits a glassy luster, slightly more brilliant than several of its pearly zeolite cousins. Calcite (page 85) is the only mineral you'll likely confuse for chabazite-(Ca). Calcite can form identical rhombohedral crystals, but a hardness test will differentiate them.

WHERE TO LOOK: The famous zeolite-bearing basalt flows near Spray, Goble, and Rainier, Oregon, are best, but old basalt quarries in Grays Harbor County, Washington, near Porter and Oakville are known for good specimens, too.

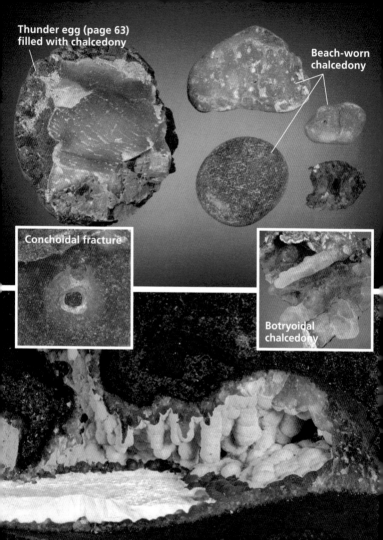

Thunder egg (page 63) filled with chalcedony

Beach-worn chalcedony

Conchoidal fracture

Botryoidal chalcedony

Chalcedony stalactites (coated in tan clay) in a basalt vesicle

Chalcedony

HARDNESS: 7 **STREAK:** White

Occurrence

ENVIRONMENT: All environments

WHAT TO LOOK FOR: Very hard, waxy masses of material displaying translucent mottled red, yellow or brown coloration

SIZE: Chalcedony masses can range from pea-sized fragments to fist-sized chunks

COLOR: Multicolored; varies greatly, but primarily mottled in shades of yellow, red, brown, green, black or gray

OCCURRENCE: Common

NOTES: Chalcedony is one of the many varieties of quartz (page 209) and is most famous as the material that composes agates (page 47). In particular, chalcedony is a variety of microcrystalline quartz, which means that instead of exhibiting the usual distinct shape of quartz crystals, chalcedony forms as irregular masses composed of countless microscopic quartz crystals. Due to chalcedony's high hardness, waxy texture, conchoidal fracture (when struck, circular cracks appear) and massive nature, the only other materials you'll likely confuse it with are other forms of microcrystalline quartz, particularly chert (page 95) and jasper (page 153). However, while the quartz microcrystals in chert and jasper are tightly compacted grains, chalcedony's microcrystals are tiny fibers arranged into parallel stacks. This makes chalcedony translucent in bright light while all but the thinnest specimens of chert and jasper are opaque. Finally, since agates consist of chalcedony, many collectors confuse the two, but a mass of chalcedony is technically only considered an agate when it contains concentric banding.

WHERE TO LOOK: Finding smoothed, weathered chalcedony is easy along the shores of Whidbey and Camano Islands in Washington and along the entire coast of Oregon.

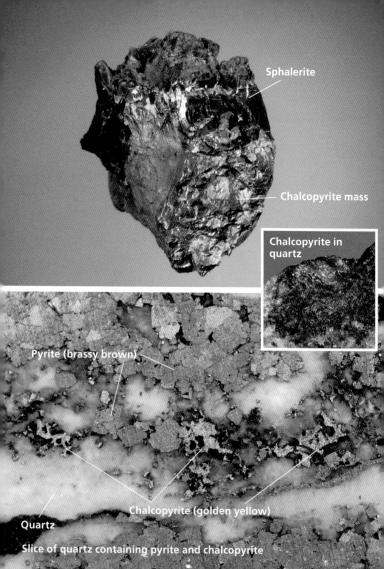

Sphalerite

Chalcopyrite mass

Chalcopyrite in quartz

Pyrite (brassy brown)

Chalcopyrite (golden yellow)

Quartz

Slice of quartz containing pyrite and chalcopyrite

Chalcopyrite

HARDNESS: 3.5–4 **STREAK:** Greenish black

Occurrence

ENVIRONMENT: Mountains, road cuts, quarries

WHAT TO LOOK FOR: Brittle, soft, brass-yellow masses or veins within rock, frequently with a bluish surface tarnish and often alongside sphalerite

SIZE: Chalcopyrite typically occurs in masses no larger than your palm and most often smaller than a pea

COLOR: Brass-yellow to golden yellow, metallic brown; sometimes with an orange, blue, purple or pink surface tarnish

OCCURRENCE: Uncommon

NOTES: A metallic mineral comprised of iron, copper and sulfur, chalcopyrite forms primarily when hot mineral-bearing volcanic water rises and deposits minerals within cavities in rock. As the most abundant copper-bearing mineral, chalcopyrite is widespread throughout the United States, though it is not particularly common in Washington and Oregon. Crystals are very rare and it more commonly forms as irregular masses embedded in rocks, particularly alongside sphalerite (page 267). Chalcopyrite appears as a bright brass-yellow metallic mineral, and it is often highly lustrous and always very brittle. This appearance is not unique, however, and chalcopyrite is easily confused with pyrite (page 203) and pyrrhotite (page 207). But of all these metallic yellow minerals, only chalcopyrite develops an orange to blue or purple surface tarnish. In addition, pyrite is much harder, while pyrrhotite will stick to a magnet and chalcopyrite will not. Chalcopyrite also weathers easily, leaving a rusty brown stain on its surroundings.

WHERE TO LOOK: Josephine County, Oregon, occasionally produces specimens along rivers, while King County, Washington, yields specimens in many mountainous locations.

Masses of chert

Mineral veins in chert

Surface detail

Chert with coral fossil impressions

Chert

HARDNESS: 7 **STREAK:** White

Occurrence

ENVIRONMENT: All environments

WHAT TO LOOK FOR: Very hard, opaque gray masses, often found on beaches as rounded pebbles with a waxy texture or as rough fragmented layers in rock formations

SIZE: Chert can occur in any size, from pebbles to boulders

COLOR: Gray to black, white or tan to brown

OCCURRENCE: Very common

NOTES: Chert is a dense, opaque sedimentary rock unique in that it consists almost entirely of quartz (page 209). Though chert can form in several different ways, most of the time it formed when sediments rich in silica (quartz compound) settled to the seafloor and were compacted. Because Washington and Oregon were once marine environments, it's understandable why chert can be found in the region, even as large cliffs. But what's most interesting about chert is the source of its silica: diatom skeletons. Diatoms are a type of algae that grow rigid skeletons formed entirely of silica. When they die, their skeletons settle at ocean bottoms to form a silica-rich silt that, in time, hardens to form chert. Sometimes found in layered formations, chert is the hardest sedimentary rock you'll find, and because it's a form of quartz, its conchoidal fracture (when struck circular cracks appear) and great hardness are distinctive features. Still, it's easy to confuse chert with other forms of quartz, like jasper (page 153), the more colorful form of chert. It can also be mistaken for chalcedony (page 91), which is translucent, and quartzite (page 213) which is grainier and glassier.

WHERE TO LOOK: Beautiful cliffs of layered chert can be seen along the Coast Range in southwestern Oregon, while small pieces can be found on shores in both states.

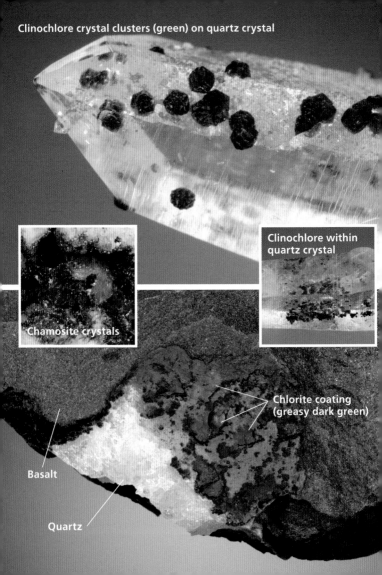

Clinochlore crystal clusters (green) on quartz crystal

Clinochlore within quartz crystal

Chamosite crystals

Chlorite coating (greasy dark green)

Basalt

Quartz

Chlorite group

HARDNESS: 2–2.5 **STREAK:** Colorless

Occurrence

ENVIRONMENT: Quarries, road cuts, mountains, fields

WHAT TO LOOK FOR: Soft, dark, "greasy" looking mineral lining the insides of gas bubbles or other surfaces on dark rocks

SIZE: Individual crystals are rare and just hundredths of an inch long; thin coatings of several inches are more common

COLOR: Light to dark green, black to brown; very rarely pink

OCCURRENCE: Massive forms are common; crystals are very rare

NOTES: The chlorite group consists of several minerals, but only two are particularly common: chamosite and clinochlore. In Washington and Oregon, clinochlore is slightly more abundant, but you won't often be able to distinguish the two minerals unless you're comparing very well-formed specimens. This makes lab tests the only way to definitively identify many specimens, and most are just labeled "chlorite." When well formed, both chamosite and clinochlore form tiny hexagonal (six-sided) plate-like crystals that are often side by side or tightly stacked, or form as globules (ball-like structures). But in even the best-crystallized specimens, strong magnification is needed, as crystals are typically just tenths or hundredths of an inch wide. Chlorite minerals usually show up as nondescript green or black linings or crusts inside vesicles (gas bubbles) in basalt, often alongside zeolite minerals such as stilbite-(Ca) (page 237). Identification can be tricky, but look for chlorite's dark green coloration, low hardness and its tendency to have a "greasy" luster.

WHERE TO LOOK: In both states, zeolite-bearing basalt vesicles are often lined with a coating of chlorite. Crystals, though extremely rare, can be found in cavities within granite at Washington Pass in Okanogan County, Washington.

Chrysocolla (blue)

Malachite crystals (green)

Chrysocolla (blue)

Malachite crystals (green)

Chrysocolla

HARDNESS: 2–4 **STREAK:** White to pale blue

ENVIRONMENT: Mountains, rivers, road cuts, quarries

Occurrence

WHAT TO LOOK FOR: Soft, blue, very crumbly or dusty crusts or masses frequently associated with malachite

SIZE: Masses are typically smaller than your thumbnail

COLOR: Light to dark blue, greenish blue

OCCURRENCE: Uncommon

NOTES: Chrysocolla is a vividly colored mineral that forms when copper-bearing minerals weather and decompose. Unlike most other minerals, chrysocolla is virtually never found in crystal form. Instead, it appears in irregular masses, chalky coatings, or botryoidal (grape-like) crusts grown atop other minerals or rocks. Chrysocolla forms in much the same way as malachite (page 171), and as a result the two minerals often occur together, and are frequently found intergrown with each other. Although chrysocolla is generally more blue in color than malachite, it can also be green, making it easy to confuse with malachite. Though malachite is typically harder than chrysocolla, the difference is often not notable enough to distinguish them. Malachite, however, frequently exhibits a fibrous structure not present in chrysocolla. In addition, chrysocolla easily desiccates (dries out) and can appear crumbly or chalky. Chrysocolla could also possibly be confused for celadonite (page 87), but celadonite is softer and normally forms within vesicles (gas bubbles) while chrysocolla rarely does.

WHERE TO LOOK: Chrysocolla can be found in small amounts in many places. Ferry and Okanogan Counties in Washington produce specimens, as do Josephine and Baker Counties in Oregon. Look along rivers where rock is weathered.

Cinnabar (red) in masses of opal

Cinnabar vein in opal

Dusty cinnabar coating (red) on opal

⚠ Cinnabar

HARDNESS: 2–2.5 **STREAK:** Red to reddish brown

Occurrence

ENVIRONMENT: Mountains, quarries, road cuts

WHAT TO LOOK FOR: Bright red crystals or coatings on the surface of other rocks or minerals, particularly quartz or opal

SIZE: Cinnabar crystals are rarely larger than a fraction of an inch, while thin coatings can measure several inches across

COLOR: Light to dark red, pink, reddish orange

OCCURRENCE: Rare

NOTES: Cinnabar is the primary ore of mercury, but don't let the notorious health effects of mercury keep you from collecting cinnabar. Because sulfur combines with mercury to form cinnabar, the mercury atoms are not entirely free to react with your skin on contact, so it is therefore safe to collect with short-term handling. Mercury poisoning becomes a possibility if you handle cinnabar for long periods without gloves, inhale its dust while collecting, ingest it, or heat cinnabar, which releases mercury fumes. But by being responsible and wary of the mineral, you can add cinnabar, one of Washington and Oregon's most colorful collectibles, to your collection. Cinnabar forms when hot volcanic water rises and deposits minerals within the rocks the water passes through. Cinnabar is therefore found sparingly in dozens of localities throughout the Cascade Range, and occurs primarily as thin crusts or coatings on the surfaces of rock or as veins within quartz or opal. Crystals exist as well, but are extremely rare and appear as tiny, brightly lustrous points. There are few other minerals you could confuse with cinnabar.

WHERE TO LOOK: Cinnabar is most abundant at old mine sites in Chelan County, Washington, south of Leavenworth. In Oregon, it can be found in basalt fissures in Clackamas County, but beware of national forest boundaries. **101**

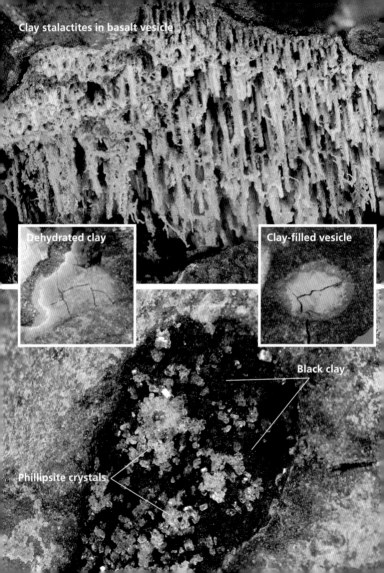

Clay stalactites in basalt vesicle

Dehydrated clay

Clay-filled vesicle

Black clay

Phillipsite crystals

Clay minerals

HARDNESS: 1–2 **STREAK:** White

Occurrence

ENVIRONMENT: Mountains, road cuts, quarries

WHAT TO LOOK FOR: Very soft, crumbly masses or crusts, often with a botryoidal (grape-like) or a stalactitic (icicle-like) structure and always chalky or earthy to the touch

SIZE: Clay mineral crystals are microscopic, but masses can range in size from fractions of an inch to several inches

COLOR: White to gray, yellow to brown, green; rarely colorless

OCCURRENCE: Very common

NOTES: Due to their often mundane and nondescript appearance, the clays are a frequently overlooked category of minerals. But given their prevalence, all rock hounds should be familiar with them. The wet, sticky mud-like material that most people associate with the word "clay" consists of a mixture of minerals and rock particles; geologically, there are a number of distinct clay minerals. Clays form as masses or crusts within cavities in weathering rocks. Zeolites form in a similar fashion, so it's not surprising that zeolites and clay minerals often occupy the same cavities, particularly vesicles (gas bubbles) in basalt. Many clay minerals are present in Washington and Oregon—montmorillonite, nontronite, saponite and kaolinite, just to name a few—but since they are almost never found crystallized (and crystals tend to be microscopic), telling them apart is nearly impossible without a lab. To identify a specimen as a clay mineral, check hardness and texture, as clays are extremely soft and chalky. Under magnification, look for botryoidal (grape-like) or rounded surface features and cracks caused by dehydration.

WHERE TO LOOK: Nearly any vesicle in zeolite-bearing basalt may contain clay minerals. Basalt formations near Goble, Oregon, and Porter, Washington, are good places to start.

Thunder eggs from central Oregon containing tiny clinoptilolite crystals

Clinoptilolite (white) in basalt vesicle

Fine clinoptilolite crystals (orange) on mordenite (white)

Clinoptilolite (red) on mordenite (white)

Clinoptilolite

HARDNESS: 3.5–4 **STREAK:** White

Occurrence

ENVIRONMENT: Quarries, road cuts, fields, rivers

WHAT TO LOOK FOR: Tiny, glassy, colorless crystals with a blocky shape within cavities in rocks like basalt and tuff

SIZE: Individual crystals are typically no larger than a few eighths of an inch; crystal groupings can measure an inch or more

COLOR: Colorless to white, pink to red or orange

OCCURRENCE: Rare

NOTES: Clinoptilolite is a member of the zeolite mineral group, a family of chemically complex hydrous (water-bearing) minerals that form within cavities in rock. Zeolites form when rock is affected by mineral-bearing groundwater. Virtually all zeolites form within basalt, so if you're looking for zeolites, start by looking for basalt. Nevertheless, clinoptilolite is also found in vesicles and cavities within andesite and rhyolite, as well as within thunder egg geodes (page 63), which formed in tuff (page 245). Clinoptilolite develops as tiny blocky, plate-like crystals, and is typically rectangular in shape with blade-like tips. But clinoptilolite is difficult to identify visually due to its similarity to heulandite-(Ca) (page 147). Not only do the two zeolites have very similar crystal shapes, colors and hardnesses, they even have the same chemical composition and only a lab can tell them apart. Your best bet for distinguishing clinoptilolite from heulandite-(Ca) is to research which of the two minerals is more common in the area where you collected. If your unidentified glassy zeolite crystals are within a thunder egg, however, you can assume it is clinoptilolite.

WHERE TO LOOK: Malheur County, Oregon, produces thunder eggs containing clinoptilolite, and basalt along the Columbia River near Rock Island, Washington, yields crystals.

Conglomerate

Water-worn breccia

Rounded stones in conglomerate

Angular fragments in breccia

Rounded pebbles

Fine-grained cement

Conglomerate

Conglomerate/Breccia

HARDNESS: N/A **STREAK:** N/A

Occurrence

ENVIRONMENT: Shoreline, rivers, quarries, fields

WHAT TO LOOK FOR: Masses of rock that appear to be made of many smaller rocks that have been cemented together

SIZE: Conglomerate and breccia can be found in any size

COLOR: Varies greatly; mottled, multicolored

OCCURRENCE: Uncommon

NOTES: Conglomerate and breccia are two sedimentary rocks that formed when smaller stones were cemented together into one large mass by fine-grained sediment. The stones within conglomerate and breccia can consist of any type of rock; their composition depends on the material that was available when the breccia or conglomerate formed. Both rocks have a rough, uneven texture and a mottled coloration. Conglomerate consists of whole stones or gravel, often rounded in shape, that are embedded within a finer grained material, such as sand. Because this type of sedimentation typically occurs in water, dissolved minerals like calcite, quartz and goethite are then able to crystallize within the spaces in the material, cementing and consolidating it into a single mass. Breccia is very similar and forms in a nearly identical manner, but consists of broken, angular fragments of rock instead of rounded pebbles. The fragments often consist of the same material, signifying that the original rock was violently crushed and then cemented back together. Since most sedimentary rocks typically have a consistent grain size, conglomerate and breccia's unique texture is apparent and differs greatly from all other rock types.

WHERE TO LOOK: Any area rich in sedimentary rock will likely yield samples, but beaches around Puget Sound in Washington and rivers in western Oregon are good places to look.

Cowlesite-lined vesicle in basalt

Ball-like growths

Cowlesite-lined vesicle in basalt

Cowlesite

HARDNESS: 5–5.5 **STREAK:** White

Occurrence

ENVIRONMENT: Rivers, quarries, road cuts

WHAT TO LOOK FOR: Vesicles (gas bubbles) in basalt lined with colorless or white crusts of ball-like crystal groupings

SIZE: Individual cowlesite "balls" are rarely larger than a few hundredths of an inch and are most often smaller

COLOR: Colorless to white, gray

OCCURRENCE: Rare

NOTES: Cowlesite is one of Washington and Oregon's many zeolite minerals. Zeolites are a group of chemically complex minerals that form in vesicles (gas bubbles) in basalt when it is affected by mineral-rich groundwater. In fact, cowlesite is one of Oregon's type locality minerals, which means that it was first discovered in the state. It is also one of the rarer zeolites of the Pacific Northwest and can be tricky to identify due to its very small size. Cowlesite forms as tiny needle-like crystals, but this is rarely observed because the crystals are always tightly intergrown into radial, ball-like aggregates. These spherical cowlesite formations are tiny, typically just a few hundredths of an inch in size, and will often line the interior of a vesicle entirely. Magnification (preferably a microscope) is crucial for both appreciating and attempting to identify cowlesite, as the ball-like aggregates will often appear "fuzzy" upon closer inspection. Unfortunately, this trait doesn't distinguish cowlesite from other zeolites, and since a hardness test isn't practical on such small specimens, you may need to seek expert advice. In particular, thomsonite-(Ca) (page 241) can form similar spherical growths, but it is much more common.

WHERE TO LOOK: In Oregon, the areas around Goble and Ritter are known localities. In Washington, try basalt near Porter.

Rock with embedded cubanite masses

Shiny cubanite

Cubanite

Embedded cubanite

Cubanite

HARDNESS: 3.5 **STREAK:** Gray-black

ENVIRONMENT: Quarries, mountains, rivers

Occurrence

WHAT TO LOOK FOR: Brassy yellow striated (grooved) metallic masses that will attract a magnet and are embedded in rock

SIZE: Masses of cubanite are generally smaller than a thumbnail

COLOR: Brass-yellow, metallic orange to brown

OCCURRENCE: Very rare

NOTES: Named for the country where it was first discovered, cubanite is a mineral that, unfortunately, very few collectors will find. In both Washington and Oregon, only a handful of mines produced the rare mineral and those areas are off-limits to collectors today. For collectors interested in finding cubanite, the only remaining hope is that specimens could be found in areas nearby the closed mines. When found, specimens typically appear as brassy yellow or metallic brown veins and masses embedded in rock. These specimens are almost never found crystallized; when they are, specimens are striated (grooved). Specimens are always magnetic, however. In fact, cubanite's magnetism is the primary way to distinguish it from its close mineralogical cousin chalcopyrite (page 93), which can resemble cubanite in nearly every other way. Cubanite's magnetism and rarity also distinguish it from pyrite (page 203), but not from pyrrhotite (page 207). Pyrrhotite is a metallic yellow or brown color and equally rare, but it can be found crystallized while cubanite crystals are almost never found in Washington or Oregon. Pyrrhotite is also generally harder and less magnetic.

WHERE TO LOOK: Cubanite was produced from private mines in the Monte Cristo area in Snohomish County, Washington, but the surrounding area may yield specimens. In Oregon, several mines in Josephine County produced cubanite.

Mordenite

Brown clay

Dachiardite crystal cluster

Loose crystal cluster

Radial crystal group

Dachiardite

HARDNESS: 4–4.5 **STREAK:** White

Occurrence

ENVIRONMENT: Road cuts, quarries

WHAT TO LOOK FOR: Small, needle-like crystals tightly intergrown in spiky or dome-like masses within cavities in basalt

SIZE: Dachiardite crystal aggregates are typically smaller than a pea, but can occasionally grow to ½ inch in width

COLOR: Colorless to white

OCCURRENCE: Rare

NOTES: Dachiardite is a zeolite mineral, and as such it forms within vesicles (gas bubbles) in basalt as the basalt is affected by water. Dachiardite also comes in two distinct varieties: a calcium-rich type known as dachiardite-(Ca) that is typically found in Oregon, and a sodium-rich type called dachiardite-(Na) that is most often found in Washington. Both are quite rare, however, and only very experienced and well-researched collectors will find them. In addition, both varieties are indistinguishable outside of a lab, so most specimens are simply labeled as dachiardite. Like many other zeolites, such as mesolite (page 175) and natrolite (page 185), dachiardite forms as thin, steeply pointed dagger-shaped crystals. Crystals are arranged into radial groupings and are sometimes so well formed that the mineral growth resembles a small dome or a ball. Unlike most similar zeolites, dachiardite's crystal groupings are often so tightly intergrown that they seemingly become a single formation. They are also frequently solid enough they can be freed from a vesicle in one piece, a rare trait among similar zeolites.

WHERE TO LOOK: In Washington, dachiardite is found in road cuts in the Altoona area along the Columbia River, south of Rosburg. In Oregon, it can be found in the area around Cape Lookout, but be mindful of state park boundaries.

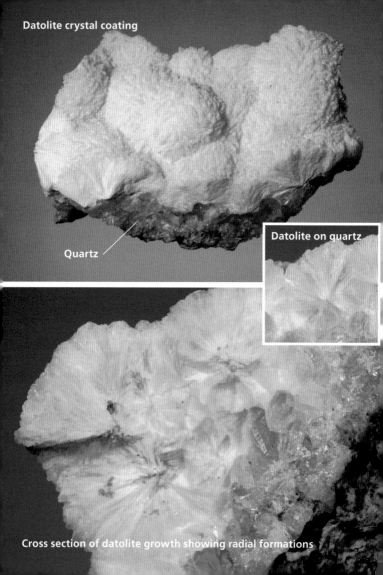

Datolite crystal coating

Quartz

Datolite on quartz

Cross section of datolite growth showing radial formations

Datolite

HARDNESS: 5–5.5 **STREAK:** White

ENVIRONMENT: Quarries, road cuts, rivers

Occurrence

WHAT TO LOOK FOR: Hard, densely intergrown radial clusters of white, porcelain-like crystals, often alongside zeolites

SIZE: Datolite clusters can measure several inches

COLOR: White to gray, pale yellow

OCCURRENCE: Rare

NOTES: Much like the many minerals of the zeolite group, datolite forms as a result of mineral-rich groundwater altering rocks, particularly basalt. As a result, it is found in vesicles (gas bubbles) and fissures in rock, often lining cavities. Elsewhere in the world, datolite typically forms as glassy transparent crystals but specimens found in Washington and Oregon take a different form. Datolite from the region occurs in veins or crusts of densely compact, opaque white radial "sprays" of slender, elongated crystals. Crystals often grow atop quartz (page 209) or alongside calcite (page 85). Unfortunately, tightly intergrown crystal groupings of some zeolites look similar, so datolite can resemble thomsonite-(Ca) (page 241) laumontite (page 161), as well as prehnite (page 201). Prehnite, however, is harder than datolite and laumontite is softer. Thomsonite-(Ca) and other similar zeolites are typically not as densely intergrown as datolite; even when they are, they tend to be more fragile and flake or crumble apart more easily, whereas datolite growths are normally quite solid. Finally, Washington and Oregon's datolite is rarer than most zeolites and tends to have a chalky feel, resembling that of unglazed porcelain.

WHERE TO LOOK: Only a few known localities exist; look in andesite and basalt formations in Lane County in Oregon and in Lewis and Skamania Counties in Washington.

115

Dolomite (pale tan) on quartz (bluish gray)

Pearly luster of dolomite crystal

Ankerite crystals

Ankerite crystal mass

Pyrite

Dolomite group

HARDNESS: 3.5–4 **STREAK:** White

Occurrence

ENVIRONMENT: Mountains, quarries, road cuts

WHAT TO LOOK FOR: Aggregates of blocky, tan or brown crystals, often with slightly curved faces and a pearly luster

SIZE: Individual crystals are rarely larger than your thumbnail while aggregates can measure several inches in size

COLOR: Tan to brown common; colorless to white uncommon

OCCURRENCE: Dolomite common; ankerite rare

NOTES: Dolomite is among the most common minerals in the world, though it is typically a constituent of sedimentary rocks and not found in a crystallized form. Dolomite and ankerite are very closely related and are the most prominent members of the dolomite group. Cousins of calcite (page 85) and siderite (page 231), both dolomite and ankerite are common minerals in sedimentary rocks, but they are only found in crystalline form within cavities in the rocks. Dolomite and ankerite each develop typically in rhombohedral crystals, which look like a cube that is tilted or leaning to one side. But unlike calcite and siderite, which also form as rhombohedrons, dolomite and ankerite often feature curving or rounded faces, often intergrown into stacks. In addition, dolomite and ankerite crystals virtually always exhibit a pearly luster and softly reflect light, while calcite is glassy and siderite is typically dull. The differences between dolomite and ankerite are more subtle, however, and without a lab, differentiating specimens is difficult. Ankerite is rarer and contains iron, so it is associated with iron-bearing minerals, such as pyrite, more often, which may help identification.

WHERE TO LOOK: Sedimentary rocks produce dolomite specimens all over Stevens County, Washington. In Oregon, dozens of locations in Grant County produce embedded specimens.

Epidote crystal cluster

Quartz

Tiny epidote crystals

Thulite veins

Thulite masses

Epidote group

HARDNESS: 6–7 **STREAK:** Colorless to gray

Occurrence

ENVIRONMENT: Mountains, road cuts, quarries,

WHAT TO LOOK FOR: Elongated green to brown striated (grooved) crystals or pink masses within metamorphic rocks

SIZE: Epidote group crystals are typically shorter than an inch; pink masses can be large, up to several inches or more

COLOR: Green to yellowish green, yellow to brown, gray, pink

OCCURRENCE: Epidote is uncommon; thulite is rare

NOTES: The epidote group is a family of hard minerals that form primarily within metamorphic rock environments. In the Pacific Northwest, the most abundant group member is epidote itself, but zoisite is present as well. Epidote is a popular collectible because it is often found well crystallized, making it easy to identify. Formed primarily in metamorphic rocks, epidote develops elongated crystals (sometimes with a fan-like shape) with deeply striated (grooved) faces and a distinct yellow-green coloration. In fact, epidote's pea-green color is so prevalent that it is often the first clue to a specimen's identity. You could confuse it with another member of the epidote family, clinozoisite (page 259), but epidote is more common and more green in color. Zoisite, a rare epidote group mineral, is found in Washington in a variety called thulite. Thulite is a massive formation composed of pink manganese-bearing zoisite and often contains spots of calcite (page 85) or pyroxenes (page 205). Though rare, it is a popular Washington collectible, typically found as veins within granite or metamorphic rocks like gneiss. Thulite can be confused with rhodonite (page 217) but is slightly harder.

WHERE TO LOOK: Epidote can be found in many places in Baker County, Oregon, while thulite can be found east of Riverside, Washington, along Tunk Creek in Okanogan County.

Tiny (1/100") erionite crystal clusters (orange) in basalt vesicles

Clinoptilolite (white)

Erionite "sprays"

Erionite (silky white) on the surfaces of plate-like crystals of levyne (gray)

Erionite

HARDNESS: 3.5–4 **STREAK:** White

Occurrence

ENVIRONMENT: Rivers, quarries, road cuts

WHAT TO LOOK FOR: Very small, delicate, needle-like crystals with a six-sided cross section within cavities in basalt

SIZE: Individual crystals are very small, rarely longer than a few eighths of an inch; groupings can be slightly larger

COLOR: Colorless to white, yellow to brown

OCCURRENCE: Very rare in Washington; rare in Oregon

NOTES: Erionite is one of Washington and Oregon's many zeolites (a group of minerals that forms in vesicles, or gas bubbles, in basalt as it is altered by water). It is found in three varieties: a calcium-rich, a potassium-rich, and a sodium-rich type. However, since there are no appreciable differences between these varieties, collectors generally just label specimens as erionite. Like many zeolites, erionite forms as tiny, delicate needle-like crystals in basalt vesicles; crystals are often arranged into divergent "spray"-shaped groupings. Yellow colorations can be distinctive, but most specimens are colorless to white and distinguishing these from other zeolites is very difficult unless you use magnification. Viewing an erionite crystal on-end should reveal a hexagonal cross section, which most other zeolites do not share. Ideal crystals are rare, however, and erionite most often occurs in epitaxial overgrowths on lévyne (page 163); this means that erionite often grows from the two flat surfaces of lévyne crystals. When viewed on-edge, specimens show a "sandwich"-like appearance of opaque white, erionite crystals on either side of a slightly darker lévyne crystal.

WHERE TO LOOK: Road cuts near Olympia, Washington, and quarries in Lincoln and Tillamook Counties in Oregon produce erionite overgrowths on lévyne and, rarely, separate crystals.

121

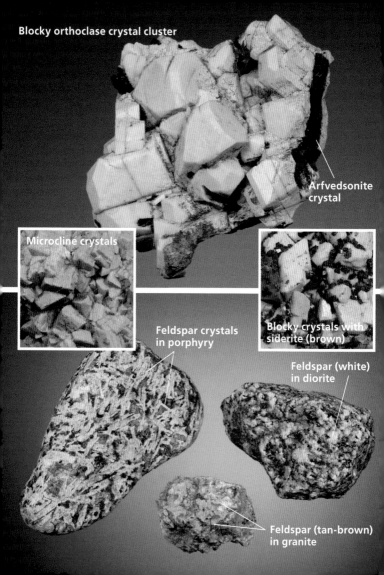

Blocky orthoclase crystal cluster

Arfvedsonite crystal

Microcline crystals

Feldspar crystals in porphyry

Blocky crystals with siderite (brown)

Feldspar (white) in diorite

Feldspar (tan-brown) in granite

Feldspar group

HARDNESS: 6–6.5 **STREAK:** White

Occurrence

ENVIRONMENT: All environments

WHAT TO LOOK FOR: Abundant, hard, light-colored masses embedded in granite, or blocky, angular crystals in cavities

SIZE: Can vary greatly in size, from specimens pea-sized and smaller to those that are several inches; feldspar masses within rocks are typically smaller than your thumbnail

COLOR: White to gray, cream-colored, yellow to brown, pink

OCCURRENCE: Very common

NOTES: The feldspars are the most abundant group of minerals and comprise nearly 60 percent of the earth's crust. Feldspars are present in virtually every type of rock and are major building blocks of the igneous rocks that underlie our world. Needless to say, it's important for rock hounds to know about feldspars. The term "feldspar" encompasses over a dozen distinct minerals that are divided into two groups: the potassium feldspars, which include orthoclase, one of the most common feldspars, and the plagioclase feldspars, which include anorthite. When well developed, all feldspars tend to form elongated, blocky, rectangular crystals with angled terminations, or tips, often intergrown in small groupings. Since crystals are rare, you'll most often find feldspar minerals as nondescript masses in rocks such as granite (page 143), or as embedded rectangular inclusions, as seen in andesite (page 71). Identification of feldspars is fairly easy because of their high hardness, blocky shapes and abundance, but identifying specific feldspars can be difficult.

WHERE TO LOOK: Masses of feldspar in granite, sometimes with occasional crystals in cavities, can be found in the Cascade Range, particularly near Washington Pass. In Oregon, road cuts near Lime in Baker County produce crystals.

Fluorapatite needles (approximately ⅟₅₀") within cavity in andesite

Close-up of tiny crystal

Fluorapatite crystal from sand (⅟₅₀")

Enstatite

Ilmenite

Fluorapatite needles (approximately ⅟₅₀")

Fluorapatite

HARDNESS: 5 **STREAK:** White

Occurrence

ENVIRONMENT: Road cuts, quarries, mountains

WHAT TO LOOK FOR: Small, glassy hexagonal (six-sided) prismatic crystals with flat tops and a moderate hardness found within cavities in rock or in sand

SIZE: Most crystals are shorter than ⅛ inch and very slender

COLOR: Colorless to white or cream-colored; rarely yellow

OCCURRENCE: Rare

NOTES: Several minerals are members of the apatite group, and though many are erroneously labeled simply as "apatite," there actually is no single mineral called apatite. Most "apatite" specimens are actually the fluorine-bearing mineral fluorapatite, the most common member of the apatite group. It develops as hexagonal prismatic crystals (six-sided crystals that are elongated in one direction). Depending on the environment in which apatite forms, it may be very thin and needle-like, or very stout. In either case, crystals typically terminate (end) with a flat tip. This crystal habit is fairly distinctive and specimens can often be identified visually, but in Washington and Oregon, fluorapatite crystals are often very small, requiring magnification. Certain localities, particularly in northwestern Oregon, produce tiny, colorless needle-like crystals that could possibly be confused with some zeolites, but these delicate fluorapatite crystals form alongside pyroxene minerals (page 205) while zeolites typically do not. Needle-like crystals can also be confused with aragonite (page 75), but aragonite is more common and its crystals are typically not hexagonal.

WHERE TO LOOK: Cavities in andesite on mountains in Klamath County, Oregon, are known for crystals, as is the area around North Bend in King County, Washington.

125

Beach-worn clam shells from Oregon's Pacific Coast

Snail shell

Turtle coprolite

Scallop shell in sandstone from Oregon's Pacific Coast

Fossils, animal

HARDNESS: N/A **STREAK:** N/A

Occurrence

ENVIRONMENT: Shoreline, rivers, fields, road cuts

WHAT TO LOOK FOR: Sedimentary rocks containing unique shapes that resemble body parts of animals

SIZE: The size of a fossil is dependent on the part of the animal that is fossilized; generally palm-sized or smaller

COLOR: Varies greatly; fossils take on the color of the surrounding rock and often appear in shades of brown, gray or green

OCCURRENCE: Uncommon

NOTES: Rock hounds often collect fossils, and animal fossils are always popular. While a fossilized fish or dinosaur may be the discovery of a collector's dreams, shells of clams and snails are a far more realistic and abundant find. Fossils form when organic matter, such as a bone or a clam shell, is buried in sediment, particularly underwater, where it cannot decay normally. Over the course of thousands or millions of years, minerals from the surrounding rock seep into the once-living organism and replace its cells, turning it into a mineral formation. This process means that only sedimentary rocks, like shale and sandstone, produce fossils. Shells are the most common of fossilized animal remains because their hard, rigid shells easily survive the fossilization process. The easiest place to find fossil shells is on Oregon's Pacific Coast where rounded lumps of brown sandstone hold fossils as white, embedded curved structures. Coprolites—fossilized dung—are a unique type of fossil found in Oregon; they can only be identified with experience.

WHERE TO LOOK: Oregon's Pacific Coast produces countless shell fossils, especially near Bandon and Newport. In Washington, the Olympic Peninsula produces fossils, particularly along rivers, as well as in the areas around Porter and Olympia.

127

Leaf and plant fossils in shale

Petrified wood

Fossil pinecone

Leaf of *metasequoia*—Oregon's state fossil

Fossils, plant

HARDNESS: N/A **STREAK:** N/A

Occurrence

ENVIRONMENT: Shoreline, rivers, fields, road cuts

WHAT TO LOOK FOR: Sedimentary rocks containing shapes or indentations that resemble plants such as ferns and leaves

SIZE: The size of a fossil is dependent on the part of the plant that is fossilized; generally palm-sized or smaller

COLOR: Varies greatly; fossils take on the color of the surrounding rock and often appear in shades of brown, gray or green.

OCCURRENCE: Uncommon

NOTES: Washington and Oregon are both famous for their fossilized plants, particularly petrified wood (page 193). An abundance of sedimentary rocks in each state means that fossils are also widespread. Like all fossils, plants fossilize when they are buried in sediment; this sediment contains little dissolved oxygen, so the plants do not decompose as they normally would. Minerals in the surrounding rock then replace the plant cells, turning them into a mineral formation. Normally this process takes place in aquatic conditions, but sometimes a volcanic eruption will bury entire forests in ash, preserving whole trees, as happened at various "petrified forests" in the Pacific Northwest. Petrified wood is often comprised of colorful jasper (page 153) and is an exciting find along rivers and Oregon's Pacific Coast. Fossilized ferns and leaves are found in between layers of shale (page 227), a sedimentary rock that can be separated with a knife.

WHERE TO LOOK: Central Washington is well known for petrified wood, particularly in the Saddle Mountain area. The Chuckanut Mountains, near Bellingham, Washington, are also known for leaf fossils in shale. In Oregon, hundreds of sites produce petrified wood, such as the areas around Paulina and Ashwood, as well as on the coast near Bandon.

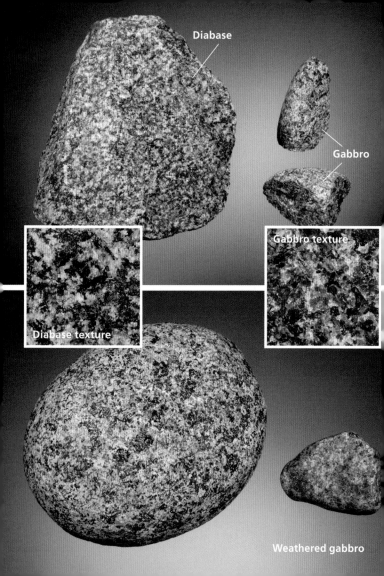

Diabase

Gabbro

Gabbro texture

Diabase texture

Weathered gabbro

Gabbro/Diabase

HARDNESS: 7 **STREAK:** White

Occurrence

ENVIRONMENT: Mountains, rivers, shoreline

WHAT TO LOOK FOR: Dark-colored, very coarsely grained rock containing many visible glassy crystals

SIZE: Gabbro and diabase both occur as huge formations of rock and can be found in any size

COLOR: Multicolored; often a mottled coloration with shades of greenish gray to black and light-colored spots; brownish when weathered

OCCURRENCE: Uncommon

NOTES: Basalt (page 83) is formed when its lava is erupted onto the earth's surface. But when it cools deep underground instead, gabbro or diabase is formed. Even though gabbro, diabase, and basalt all have the same mineral composition, they are easy to distinguish thanks to their grain size and appearance. Unlike basalt, gabbro contains large crystals; these crystals formed as it slowly cooled. Their large size makes it easy to see the plagioclase feldspar, olivine, pyroxene, magnetite and other crystallized dark minerals that make up the rock. There aren't a lot of gabbro outcroppings in the Pacific Northwest and this helps collectors identify its mottled coloration amid other coarse-grained rocks, like granite (page 143). Light-colored gabbro may closely resemble diorite (page 249), but gabbro contains virtually no quartz (page 209), which is a key trait. If the rock cools closer to the earth's surface, diabase results. Finer grained than gabbro, diabase more closely resembles basalt, but has larger embedded grains of light-colored feldspar (page 123).

WHERE TO LOOK: Gabbro and diabase can be found sparingly throughout the Cascade Mountain Range, but specimens are more easily accessed on shores and in rivers.

Intergrown garnets on skarn

Diamond-shaped crystal face

Loose water-worn garnets

Garnet in schist

Intergrown grossular

Grossular on quartz

Grossular garnet on skarn

Diopside

Garnet group

HARDNESS: 6.5–7.5 **STREAK:** Colorless

Occurrence

ENVIRONMENT: All environments

WHAT TO LOOK FOR: Very hard crystals resembling faceted balls, often embedded in schist or as loose grains in sand

SIZE: Garnets are typically smaller than a pea, but can rarely grow to several inches in width

COLOR: Red to brown common; yellow to green, pink to orange

OCCURRENCE: Common in Washington; uncommon in Oregon

NOTES: The garnet group encompasses well over a dozen different minerals that all share a similar molecular structure and crystal shape. The most common garnets in the Pacific Northwest are grossular and almandine, both of which form as dodecahedrons, or twelve-faced crystals that take on a ball-like shape. Each face on these crystals is pentagonal (five-sided), or, in certain cases, four-sided and shaped like a diamond. These shapes alone are often enough to identify a specimen as a garnet, but identifying a specific garnet variety is often impossible outside a lab. Unfortunately, not all garnets are well formed. When attempting to identify poorly formed crystals or irregular masses, garnet's common reddish brown coloration will be a clue, as will its high hardness. Garnets typically form as a result of metamorphic activity and are therefore common within schist (page 137) and skarn (page 233). Finally, because garnets are so hard and weather resistant, they can often be found in rivers or as tiny grains in sand.

WHERE TO LOOK: Beach sand at Port Townsend, Washington, yields tiny crystals, but larger, intergrown crystals are found in skarn near Vesper Peak in Snohomish County, but beware of national forest boundaries. In Oregon, schists in Coos County produce small embedded crystals.

Broken geode

Chalcedony lining (white)

Clay (tan)

Whole geode

Same specimen as above under short-wave ultraviolet light showing fluorescent green chalcedony

Geodes

HARDNESS: N/A **STREAK:** N/A

Occurrence

ENVIRONMENT: Mountains, quarries, road cuts, rivers, fields

WHAT TO LOOK FOR: Round bodies of rock with hollow centers, often containing minerals such as quartz within

SIZE: Most geodes are generally smaller than a grapefruit

COLOR: Externally, brown to gray or green; internally, varies greatly, often white, gray or multicolored

OCCURRENCE: Uncommon

NOTES: A geode is any round rock or mineral formation with a hollow center. That may seem a rather broad definition, but geodes are a broad subject; geodes can consist of many different materials and form in a variety of different geological environments. For example, some agates (page 47) are geodes and contain a hollow void at their center. Most geodes, however, are formed of rock and appear as mundane ball-like masses with lumpy, irregular surfaces when whole. But geodes are much more exciting when they are cut or broken open, revealing the cavity inside. That's because various minerals can form within geodes; the most common linings are quartz crystals or chalcedony (page 91). Other geode-filling minerals include varieties of opal (page 191) and even rare zeolites like clinoptilolite (page 105). Thunder eggs (page 63) are locally considered geodes even though most are not actually hollow. Identifying a whole, unbroken geode is difficult, but searching for abnormally round, hard rocks, particularly those embedded in clay or other soft material, is a good start.

WHERE TO LOOK: Thunder eggs, many of which are hollow, are found near Madras, Oregon. In Washington, geodes can be found in the Walker Valley area, near Mount Vernon.

Granitic gneiss

Diorite gneiss

Talc schist

Garnet in weathered mica schist

Various schists

Layered minerals

Gneiss/Schist

HARDNESS: N/A **STREAK:** N/A

Occurrence

ENVIRONMENT: Mountains, shoreline, rivers

WHAT TO LOOK FOR: Hard layered or banded rocks, often containing embedded pockets of very hard minerals

SIZE: Specimens of gneiss and schist can be found in any size

COLOR: Varies; often multicolored gray to black, white or brown

OCCURRENCE: Common

NOTES: When a body of rock is subjected to great heat and/or pressure, it undergoes chemical changes in a process called metamorphism. Many rocks that undergo metamorphosis partially melt and turn to a semi-solid state. In the process their mineral grains are rearranged and compressed into layers. Gneiss (pronounced "nice") and schist are general terms for rocks that have undergone this process to varying degrees. Gneiss is traditionally defined as a rock with less than half of its minerals arranged into layers, thereby retaining much of the original rock's appearance. Varieties of gneiss are typically labelled according to the original rock; for example, granitic gneiss originally began as granite and exhibits many of granite's characteristics. Conversely, schist is the label given to metamorphic rocks that have had more than half of their minerals compressed into layers. In schists, the original material has been changed so extensively that its minerals no longer match the original rock. For this reason, schists are named for the primary mineral within them; mica schist, for example, is particularly common and consists primarily of micas (page 177). To identify gneiss and schist, look for dense, compact rocks with colored layers or bands.

WHERE TO LOOK: To find samples of gneiss and schist, look on the coasts of both states; hunt along beaches or on riverbanks where the specimens are weathered.

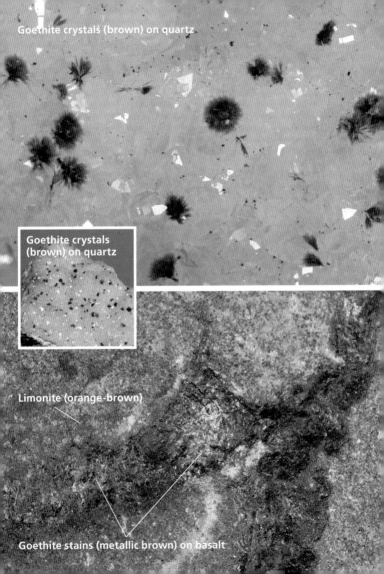

Goethite crystals (brown) on quartz

Goethite crystals (brown) on quartz

Limonite (orange-brown)

Goethite stains (metallic brown) on basalt

Goethite

Occurrence

HARDNESS: 5–5.5 **STREAK:** Yellow-brown

ENVIRONMENT: Mountains, quarries, road cuts, fields, rivers

WHAT TO LOOK FOR: A metallic brown mineral, often as a dull rust-colored crust or stain on rocks; more rarely found as radiating masses composed of thin, needle-like crystals

SIZE: Most goethite specimens are smaller than a fist

COLOR: Black to brown, yellow-brown to rust-brown, orange

OCCURRENCE: Uncommon

NOTES: Like hematite (page 145), goethite (pronounced "ger-tite") is an iron oxide mineral and consists of a combination of iron, oxygen and water. Unlike hematite, however, collector-quality specimens of goethite are not common. Goethite is essentially the same material as rust, and is the primary constituent of limonite (page 167). As such, it is most abundant as chalky yellow-brown coatings or stains on rocks and other minerals. But when it is found crystallized, the resulting specimens are often beautiful and take the form of radial arrangements of brown, metallic, needle-like crystals, often on or within quartz (page 209). Sometimes these crystal groupings are so intergrown that they appear spherical and "fuzzy," but most are very small. When formed massively, goethite often exhibits a fibrous structure, but it can still look very similar to hematite and magnetite (page 169); hematite's streak is reddish while goethite's is much more yellow in color. Magnetite is strongly magnetic and will cling to a magnet while goethite will not.

WHERE TO LOOK: King County, Washington, has produced crystallized specimens, as has Walker Valley in Skagit County. In Oregon, specimens have been found in basalt along the Clackamas River in Clackamas County.

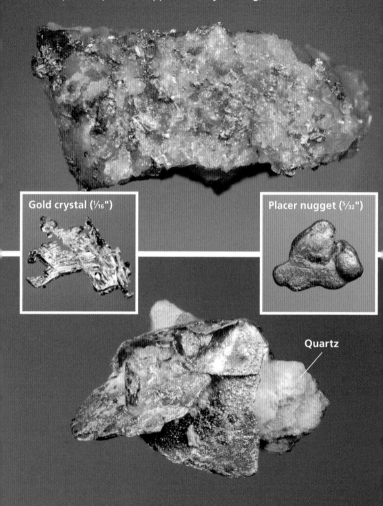

Gold in quartz (specimen approximately ¼" long)

Gold crystal (1/16")

Placer nugget (5/32")

Quartz

Flat gold crystals (specimen approximately ⅛" long)

Gold

HARDNESS: 2.5 **STREAK:** Golden yellow

Occurrence

ENVIRONMENT: Rivers, mountains

WHAT TO LOOK FOR: Tiny flecks and grains of bright yellow, highly malleable metallic material embedded within quartz or as loose nuggets at river bottoms

SIZE: Gold specimens are very rarely larger than a pea

COLOR: Metallic yellow

OCCURRENCE: Very rare

NOTES: Throughout most of history, no metal has been more desirable or valuable than gold. Gold is a native element, which means it is found uncombined with any other elements. As a pure metal, it exhibits traits that no other mineral will share, making identification simple. Gold is deposited primarily as a result of hydrothermal activity, when volcanic activity causes hot, mineral-bearing water to rise from deep within the earth. This process typically deposits gold as tiny flakes and veins within masses of quartz, making it extremely difficult to free the gold. But when gold is freed naturally, it often ends up as pure nuggets or flakes at the bottom of rivers. This is called placer (pronounced "plasser") gold and is the primary way collectors find specimens. Because gold is so dense, even the tiniest grains sink and are often trapped around boulders on river bottoms. However you find a specimen, its color is the first clue to its identity. Gold does not corrode, so it is always found in its famous bright yellow color. Though pyrite (page 203), often called "fool's gold," can look similar, gold is much rarer, is malleable (bendable), and is much softer.

WHERE TO LOOK: There are few accessible locations where gold is available, but rivers in volcanic areas, particularly rivers in or near mountains, are worth a look.

Various granites

Close-up of texture

Common coloration

Weathered granite

Granite

HARDNESS: N/A **STREAK:** N/A

Occurrence

ENVIRONMENT: Mountains, rivers, shoreline, road cuts, quarries

WHAT TO LOOK FOR: Very coarse-grained rock containing many differently colored, easily visible grains of different minerals

SIZE: Granite can be any size, from pebbles to mountains

COLOR: Varies greatly; multicolored white to gray, black, yellow to tan or orange, brown, occasionally with red areas

OCCURRENCE: Very common

NOTES: Granite makes up almost all of the rock underlying earth's continents and provides a perfect visual example of how minerals come together to form a rock. An igneous rock, granite forms when molten rock cools and hardens, but unlike other igneous rocks, such as rhyolite (page 219), granite formed deep within the earth rather than on the earth's surface. Because granite formed within the earth, it cooled very slowly and the individual minerals within it grew to a large, visible size. Granite is composed primarily of quartz, potassium feldspars, amphiboles and micas, making it largely light-colored and typically quite hard. Each spot of color in granite is a different mineral, giving granite its mottled coloration. By comparison, even though rhyolite is made up of nearly the exact same minerals as granite, it cooled on the earth's surface and hardened rapidly. Consequently, the minerals within it are very small-grained. Granite's coarse-grained appearance makes it easy to identify, as other similarly colored rocks are finer grained.

WHERE TO LOOK: The abundance of granite at Washington Pass in Okanogan County, Washington, and the rare minerals that can sometimes be found within it, make it a destination. Elsewhere, almost any river produces rounded samples.

143

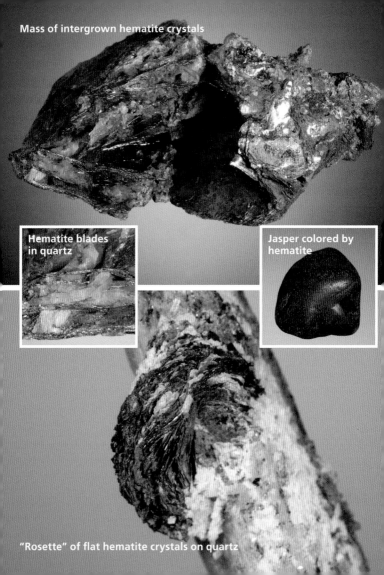

Mass of intergrown hematite crystals

Hematite blades in quartz

Jasper colored by hematite

"Rosette" of flat hematite crystals on quartz

Hematite

Occurrence

HARDNESS: 5–6 **STREAK:** Reddish brown

ENVIRONMENT: Mountains, road cuts, rivers, quarries

WHAT TO LOOK FOR: Dark gray metallic mineral, often with a reddish brown surface coloration and flat, plate-like crystals

SIZE: Hematite crystals are typically smaller than an inch, but masses of hematite can be found up to a foot or larger

COLOR: Steel gray to black; often with reddish or brown surfaces

OCCURRENCE: Common

NOTES: Hematite is a simple mixture of iron and oxygen and the most abundant iron ore on earth. As it is so abundant and occurs in so many environments, it can take many forms. Hematite crystals, though rare, form as metallic, gray, flat, hexagonal (six-sided) discs, but crudely formed plates lacking a well-defined crystal structure are more abundant. Botryoidal (grape-like) masses are more common than either of these growth habits; botryoidal masses often lack the metallic luster and are instead coated with a dull brown material. However, thin crusts on other rocks or minerals or massive formations with no distinct shape are most abundant of all. In most cases, hematite is associated with red dusty coatings that form when hematite weathers. This red is also hematite's streak color, which differentiates it from goethite (page 139), another iron mineral that can look like hematite, but which has a yellowish brown streak. In fact, you can assume hematite is present in any rock with a reddish coloration. Ilmenite (page 149) and magnetite (page 169) can also resemble metallic black hematite, but both of those are magnetic while hematite is not.

WHERE TO LOOK: Several mountainous locations in King County, Washington, produce crystals. In Oregon, andesite mountains in Klamath County produces tiny but perfect crystals.

145

Heulandite-(Ca) specimens

Small intergrown crystals

Crystal-lined cavity

Large crystal on matrix

Single large crystal

Crystal on mordenite

Mass of intergrown crystals

Heulandite-(Ca)

HARDNESS: 3.5–4 **STREAK:** White

Occurrence

ENVIRONMENT: Rivers, quarries, road cuts

WHAT TO LOOK FOR: Small plate-like crystals found within vesicles (gas bubbles) in basalt; crystals are widest at their center

SIZE: Individual crystals are small, rarely larger than a thumbnail

COLOR: Colorless to white or gray, cream-colored to pink, yellow to brown, rarely green or red

OCCURRENCE: Uncommon

NOTES: Washington and Oregon are famous for zeolites, a group of minerals that form within cavities in basalt or andesite as the rock is affected by mineral-rich alkaline groundwater. Heulandite-(Ca) is one of the most widespread zeolites. Two varieties of heulandite are actually present in the Pacific Northwest: a potassium-rich variety called heulandite-(K) that is very rare, and the much more common calcium-rich variety, heulandite-(Ca). Since they form identical crystals and can't be distinguished without access to a lab, you can safely assume that any specimens you find are heulandite-(Ca). Heulandite-(Ca) forms in plate-like crystals that are often described as taking the shape of an old-fashioned coffin; crystals are widest at their center and have a flat tip. This shape is so distinctive and present so often that it's normally the only distinguishing feature needed for identification. If a specimen has imperfect crystals, heulandite-(Ca) could be confused for calcite (page 85), which is softer, apophyllite-(KF) (page 73), which is harder, or stilbite-(Ca) (page 237), which forms crystals with a very different shape.

WHERE TO LOOK: There are many localities, but basalt in Cowlitz and Skamania Counties in Washington is very lucrative. In Oregon, try basalt in Goble and Rainier, in Columbia County.

Enstatite crystal

Hexagonal ilmenite crystal (³⁄₆₄") in andesite cavity

Ilmenite-bearing magnetic river sand

Bluish ilmenite in gabbro

Hexagonal ilmenite crystal (¹⁄₁₆") in andesite cavity

Ilmenite

HARDNESS: 5–6   **STREAK:** Brownish black

Occurrence

ENVIRONMENT: Mountains, road cuts, quarries

WHAT TO LOOK FOR: Brittle, weakly magnetic, black metallic hexagonal (six-sided) crystals or masses embedded in rock

SIZE: Ilmenite crystals are generally smaller than ⅛ inch wide and embedded masses are normally smaller than a pea

COLOR: Metallic black, bluish; brownish black when weathered

OCCURRENCE: Uncommon; crystals are very rare

NOTES: Ilmenite is an ore of titanium that typically occurs only as nondescript black, metallic grains or masses embedded within dark rocks like basalt and gabbro. But luckily for rock hounds in the Pacific Northwest, Washington and Oregon are both home to localities that produce rare crystals of ilmenite. When crystallized, ilmenite forms small, thin, plate-like crystals with a hexagonal shape very similar to those of hematite (page 145). Unlike hematite, ilmenite is weakly magnetic and will loosely bond with a magnet. Mountains in Klamath County, Oregon, are famous for ilmenite crystals that form within cavities in andesite (page 71) alongside other rare minerals. Irregular masses of ilmenite can be distinguished from hematite by checking for magnetism, but magnetite (page 169) can resemble ilmenite and is also magnetic. But where ilmenite is merely attracted to a magnet, magnetite will bond strongly with one, even moving across a table's surface due to a magnetic attraction. In addition, ilmenite exhibits conchoidal fracture (when struck, circular cracks appear) while magnetite does not. Finally, ilmenite, along with magnetite, is a primary constituent of black sand.

WHERE TO LOOK: Summit Peak in Klamath County, Oregon, produces small but perfect crystals in andesite. In Washington, cavities in granite at Washington Pass produce crystals.

Large mass of water-worn nephrite jade

Cut nephrite from Whidbey Island, WA

Polished nephrite

Mass of jadeite

Jade

HARDNESS: 5–6 **STREAK:** White

Occurrence

ENVIRONMENT: Shorelines, rivers, road cuts

WHAT TO LOOK FOR: Hard, greenish masses, often rounded by water and exhibiting mottled, streaked coloration

SIZE: Masses of jade are typically smaller than your fist, but some specimens can measure several feet in size

COLOR: Light to dark green, gray-green to white

OCCURRENCE: Nephrite jade is uncommon; jadeite is rare

NOTES: Used in carvings and jewelry for centuries, jade is a popular collectible all along the Pacific Coast of the U.S. and Canada, and many people are familiar with it. But most people don't know that jade isn't a distinct mineral and that the term "jade" actually encompasses two completely different minerals: actinolite (page 45) and jadeite. Nevertheless, due to their similar properties, actinolite and jadeite have been referred to as jade since antiquity. These minerals are referred to as jade when they form in dense, tightly compact masses instead of crystals. Jade formed of actinolite is commonly called nephrite jade and is much more common than jadeite, especially on Washington and Oregon's shores. Jadeite, which is not found in Oregon, is a member of the pyroxene group of minerals (page 205) and is quite rare in Washington. While the two varieties are difficult to distinguish from each other due to their similar hardness, jade is generally easy to identify thanks to its color, its massive nature, and because it primarily occurs as rounded stones on beaches. Jade is also softer than similarly colored jaspers (page 153).

WHERE TO LOOK: The Pacific Coast of both states is well known for beach-worn nephrite. Jadeite is only found in Washington, particularly in Skagit County.

Water-worn jaspers from the Washington and Oregon coasts

Close-up of texture

Polished jasper from Dry Creek, OR

Rough mass of "McDermitt" jasper from southeastern Oregon

"Black" jasper from Wasco, OR

Jasper

HARDNESS: 7 **STREAK:** White

ENVIRONMENT: All environments

Occurrence

WHAT TO LOOK FOR: Very hard, opaque masses of brown or reddish material, often with a waxy feel and appearance

SIZE: Masses of jasper can be found in any size, but collected specimens are typically no larger than an adult's fist

COLOR: Varies greatly; typically mottled and multicolored, ranging from red to orange, yellow to brown, or green

OCCURRENCE: Very common

NOTES: Jasper is the name given to colorful varieties of chert (page 95), a variety of microcrystalline quartz (page 209). Jasper consists of countless microscopic quartz crystals, and therefore has no crystal structure of its own. Instead, it takes the shape of its surroundings during formation. Like any form of quartz, jasper is extremely hard and resistant to weathering. In fact, jasper is so hard that not even a steel knife will scratch it. Jasper exhibits a waxy, semi-shiny appearance and texture when smoothed by wind, water or ice, but when freshly exposed or broken, jasper often has a rough, ragged and dull appearance. Thanks to jasper's great hardness and its conchoidal fracture (when struck, circular cracks appear), it's easy to identify it as a variety of quartz. You're only likely to confuse it with chert and chalcedony (page 91). To determine if your specimen is jasper, examine its opacity and color. Chalcedony, another form of microcrystalline quartz, has a more organized structure and is translucent, whereas chert and jasper are opaque. Finally, jasper is colored shades of red, brown and green by iron-bearing minerals, but chert is typically gray or black.

WHERE TO LOOK: Beaches are the easiest place to find jasper and virtually any shoreline in both states will yield specimens.

153

"Marston" jasper · "Willow Creek" jasper · "Blue Mountain" jasper

Slabs of fancy jasper

"Gary Green" or "Larsonite" jasper

"Carrasite" jasper

"Cherry Creek" jasper

Polished specimen of museum-quality "Morrisonite" jasper

Specimen courtesy of
Eugene Mueller

Jasper, fancy

HARDNESS: 7 **STREAK:** White

Occurrence

ENVIRONMENT: All environments

WHAT TO LOOK FOR: Very hard, opaque masses of brown or reddish material, often found as veins within rock

SIZE: Masses of jasper can be found in any size, but collected specimens are typically no larger than an adult's fist

COLOR: Varies greatly; typically mottled and multicolored, ranging from red to orange, yellow to brown, or green; often with colored stripes

OCCURRENCE: Uncommon in Oregon; rare in Washington

NOTES: Not all jasper is plainly colored and otherwise feature-less—some specimens contain wildly sweeping layered patterns and beautiful color variations. Traditionally, these more exciting varieties are called "fancy jasper" and they are frequently used in jewelry. Oregon is particularly famous for its jasper varieties, many of which were named for the location where they are found or their discoverer. For example, "Owyhee" picture jasper, from the Owyhee River area, is typically tan to blue and often has attractive streaks of red and orange created when iron-bearing water stained cracks in the jasper. Other fancy jaspers contain curving layers of color that resemble landscapes; these are known as "picture" jaspers (page 159). "Polka dot" jasper is another popular type and contains orbs of color. To identify fancy jas-per, look for the familiar traits of common jasper (page 153), plus the addition of unique colors and patterns. Some jasper varieties are misnomers; the popular "spider web" jasper, for example, is actually a type of green rhyolite (page 219).

WHERE TO LOOK: Most fancy jaspers are found in eastern Oregon, particularly near the Idaho border, and in north-central Oregon, such as along the Deschutes River.

"Spider" jasper

"Polka dot" jasper

"Paiute" jasper

Slabs of jasper varieties

"Amethyst Sage" jasper

Orbicular jasper

"Kaleidoscope" jasper

"Wascoite" jasper

"Sheep Creek" jasper

"Bat Cave" jasper

Unpolished jaspers

Jasper, named varieties

HARDNESS: 7 **STREAK:** White

Occurrence

ENVIRONMENT: All environments

WHAT TO LOOK FOR: Very hard, opaque masses of brown or reddish material, often formed as veins within rock

SIZE: Masses of jasper can be found in any size, but collected specimens are typically no larger than an adult's fist

COLOR: Varies greatly; typically mottled and multicolored red to orange, yellow to brown, or green

OCCURRENCE: Very common in Oregon; common in Washington

NOTES: Dozens of different colorations and patterns can be found within the Pacific Northwest's jaspers, each of which is often considered to be a different variety of jasper. You'll hear all kinds of names applied to jasper, most of which reference the locality where a variety is found, the person who discovered it, or the appearance of the jasper. "Wascoite," for example, is a tan variety that contains layering and is found near Wasco, Oregon, while "Morrisonite," a dark green segmented and banded variety, is named after its discoverer. Sometimes, these local names can seem arbitrary—occasionally, seemingly identical specimens of jasper will have two different names simply because they came from different sides of the same formation—but they are very important to the region's jasper collectors as they denote exactly where a specimen originated. But there are varieties whose names are scientific, too. Orbicular jasper, for example, contains many small spherical formations.

WHERE TO LOOK: There are many locations; dozens of locations in Oregon produce jasper, particularly along rivers on the Idaho border and near the Deschutes River and Biggs Junction on the Washington border. Beaches along Puget Sound in Washington also produce colorful striped jaspers.

157

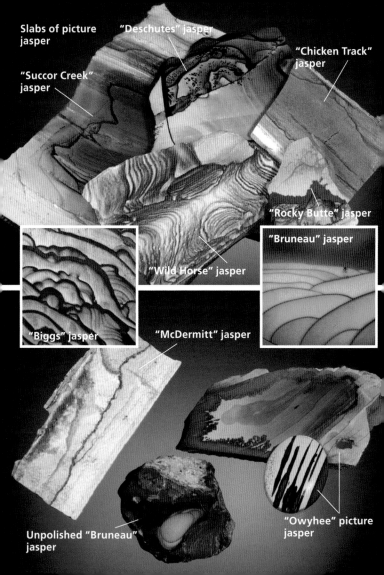

Slabs of picture jasper

"Deschutes" jasper

"Chicken Track" jasper

"Succor Creek" jasper

"Rocky Butte" jasper

"Bruneau" jasper

"Wild Horse" jasper

"Biggs" jasper

"McDermitt" jasper

"Owyhee" picture jasper

Unpolished "Bruneau" jasper

Jasper, picture

HARDNESS: 7 **STREAK:** White

Occurrence

ENVIRONMENT: All environments

WHAT TO LOOK FOR: Very hard, opaque masses of brown or reddish banded or layered material, often as veins within rock

SIZE: Masses of jasper can be found in any size, but collected specimens are typically no larger than an adult's fist

COLOR: Varies greatly; typically mottled and multicolored, ranging from red to orange, yellow to brown or green, often with stripes of color

OCCURRENCE: Uncommon in Oregon; rare in Washington

NOTES: "Picture" jaspers are some of the most desirable jaspers in the Pacific Northwest. These jaspers exhibit curving, rounded, almost agate-like layers of color that look like paintings of landscape scenes, giving them their colloquial name. Many picture jaspers form due to the silicification of sediment or rock; this occurs when dissolved silica (quartz material) saturates the material and hardens into a mass of microgranular quartz. The patterns in picture jaspers are created due to the flowing movement of the sediment from which they formed. "Biggs" jasper, from the area near Biggs Junction, Oregon, is a perfect example of this. It developed its flow-patterned appearance when basalt (page 83) lava entered a lake, trapping sediment beneath it. Other jaspers get their patterns from flows of volcanic ash or mud. Most specimens of picture jasper are easy to identify, especially when cut and polished. If you find some, take note of where you found it, as this is important information for collectors.

WHERE TO LOOK: Most of the best jaspers are found in eastern Oregon, particularly near the Idaho border, and in north-central Oregon, such as along the Deschutes River. Jaspers can be found in southeastern Washington as well.

Intergrown laumontite crystals

Steeply terminated crystal

Laumontite (white) in basalt

Intergrown laumontite crystals

Laumontite

HARDNESS: 4 **STREAK:** White

Occurrence

ENVIRONMENT: Rivers, quarries, road cuts

WHAT TO LOOK FOR: Very brittle, elongated, light-colored crystals with flat, steeply angled tips; found within cavities in basalt

SIZE: Individual crystals are often thinner than ⅛ inch but can be up to 1 inch long; crystal groupings can be several inches

COLOR: Colorless to white, cream-colored, pink or light brown

OCCURRENCE: Uncommon

NOTES: Washington and Oregon contain enormous amounts of basalt, the dark, dense volcanic rock that forms ocean floors. When basalt is affected by alkaline water, new minerals often begin to form within vesicles (gas bubbles) in the rock. This is how laumontite forms; it is just one of the dozens of related minerals in the zeolite group, which all form in a similar manner. Laumontite has elongated rectangular crystals that terminate (are tipped) with steeply angled, but flat, faces. Crystals are often intergrown in large, "tangled" groupings. Though laumontite is actually more closely related to analcime (page 69), most collectors are likely to confuse it with two similar-looking minerals, natrolite (page 185) or perhaps apophyllite-(KF) (page 73), a non-zeolite mineral. But laumontite is easy to identify thanks to one unfortunate trait: laumontite easily dehydrates, or loses water. Very fresh specimens are glassy and translucent, but the longer they are exposed to air, the more specimens become duller, more opaque and chalkier. In addition, dehydrated specimens are extremely brittle and will crumble. Finally, some specimens are weakly fluorescent.

WHERE TO LOOK: Basalt around Rainier and Kalama in Cowlitz County, Washington, are known for good specimens, as are basalt quarries near Drain in Douglas County, Oregon.

161

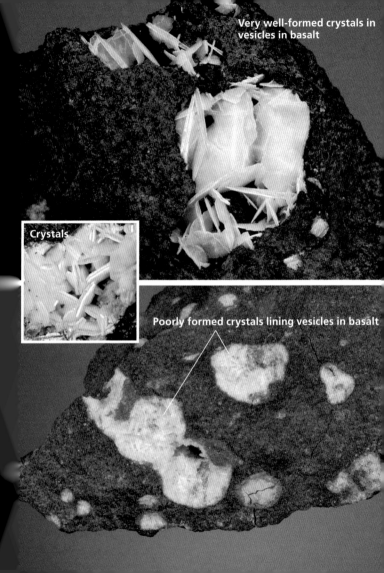

Very well-formed crystals in vesicles in basalt

Crystals

Poorly formed crystals lining vesicles in basalt

Lévyne

HARDNESS: 4–4.5 **STREAK:** White

Occurrence

ENVIRONMENT: Quarries, road cuts

WHAT TO LOOK FOR: Very small, thin, hexagonal (six-sided) plate-like crystals on the walls of vesicles (gas bubbles) in basalt

SIZE: Individual crystals of lévyne are always smaller than ¼ inch

COLOR: Colorless to white or gray

OCCURRENCE: Rare

NOTES: Lévyne (pronounced "leh-VEEN") gets its peculiar name from the French mineralogist who studied it in the 1800s. It is one of Washington and Oregon's many zeolite minerals. The zeolites formed when basalt was affected by alkaline water; the basalt weathered to form new minerals within vesicles (gas bubbles) and other cavities in the rock. There are well over a dozen zeolites present in the Pacific Northwest, and lévyne is not only one of the most uncommon, but one of the most unique and distinctive. Its white crystals are very rarely larger than ⅛ inch, and this small crystal size may initially hinder identification, possibly causing one to mistake lévyne for laumontite (page 161). But with some magnification, lévyne can be identified visually without the need for other tests. Its crystals are hexagonal, or six-sided, and very flat. These tiny disc-like crystals typically stand on edge; upon much closer inspection, you may notice that the edges of some crystals may vary in color, and are slightly darker in the middle. This sandwich-like appearance is due to overgrowths of erionite (page 121), another zeolite, with the lévyne actually at the center.

WHERE TO LOOK: Reliable localities are rare, but basalt formations near Spray in Wheeler County, Oregon, are known for specimens. In Washington, try outcrops of vesicular basalt in Thurston County southwest of Olympia.

Close-up of texture

Dirty, impurity-rich limestone

Limestone

HARDNESS: 3–4 **STREAK:** N/A

Occurrence

ENVIRONMENT: Shoreline, road cuts, fields, quarries

WHAT TO LOOK FOR: Soft, light-colored rock that has a chalky feel and is more abundant in flatter, low-lying areas

SIZE: Limestone can occur in any size, from pebbles to cliffs

COLOR: White to gray or dark gray, yellow to brown, reddish

OCCURRENCE: Common

NOTES: Limestone is a sedimentary rock that formed in marine conditions. Given the proximity of the Pacific Ocean, it is a fairly common rock in the region. Other sedimentary rocks, like sandstone (page 221) and mudstone (page 183), are more common, but limestone is still an important rock to understand. Limestone forms at the bottom of seas when the remains of microscopic organisms settle and condense into large beds. It consists of more than 50 percent calcite (page 85), but limestone also contains small amounts of clay, dolomite and quartz. Due to its high calcite content, limestone, like calcite, will effervesce, or fizz, in acid and even a single drop of vinegar will be enough to start a reaction. This trait alone will help you identify a specimen. Limestone is typically white or gray in color, often with a chalky white appearance and a chalky texture where worn, but can be yellow, brown or even reddish depending on the amount of iron-bearing minerals contained within it. And thanks to its aquatic origins, fossils are particularly common within limestone. Finally, a variety of limestone called dolostone contains dolomite (page 117), not calcite, as its primary constituent.

WHERE TO LOOK: Washington's San Juan Island is composed largely of limestone, as is the Metaline Falls area. In Oregon, it is prevalent in Baker County, especially near Huntington.

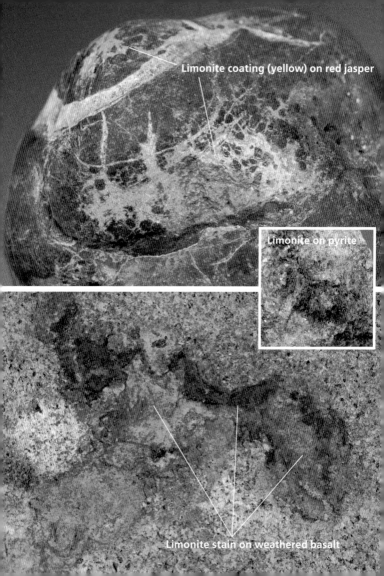

Limonite coating (yellow) on red jasper

Limonite on pyrite

Limonite stain on weathered basalt

Limonite

HARDNESS: 4–5.5 **STREAK:** Yellowish brown

Occurrence

ENVIRONMENT: Mountains, fields, road cuts, quarries, rivers

WHAT TO LOOK FOR: Chalky yellow-brown irregular masses or crusts with no discernible crystal structure

SIZE: Limonite can be found in any size, though masses or crusts are typically smaller than a few inches

COLOR: Yellow to brown, rust-colored to orange, less commonly dark brown to black

OCCURRENCE: Very common

NOTES: Limonite is not actually a mineral; instead, it is the generalized name given to unidentified granular mixtures of hydrous iron oxide minerals (grains of minerals composed of a water-bearing combination of iron and oxygen). Limonite forms as chalky, earthy masses or crusts on the surface of rocks or other minerals. Grains of limonite can also be found embedded in rocks like sandstone, due to weathering of other iron-bearing minerals. Goethite (page 139) is the primary mineral within limonite, and it typically takes on goethite's yellow-brown hues and streak color. Because of these similarities, it's easy to mistake limonite for goethite. Nevertheless, limonite is much more common, and goethite exhibits a fibrous structure whereas limonite has no structure at all. Finding limonite is as simple as looking for rusty iron stains or crusts on rocks, in soil, or on other minerals, like siderite (page 231) and pyrite (page 203). Pyrite specimens that have decomposed into limonite are one of the most unique varieties; they look brown instead of brassy.

WHERE TO LOOK: Limonite can be found almost anywhere if you look hard enough. Rare specimens of limonite replacing pyrite can be found in King County, Washington.

Pink garnets

Magnified magnetite crystal (approximately 1/80") in river sand

Magnetite in gabbro

Crystal (1/80") on epidote

Black magnetic river sand containing magnetite and ilmenite

Magnetite

HARDNESS: 5.5–6.5 **STREAK:** Black

Occurrence

ENVIRONMENT: All environments

WHAT TO LOOK FOR: Metallic black, hard, magnetic pyramid-shaped crystals, or masses or grains embedded in rocks

SIZE: Specimens of magnetite, crystallized or not, are typically smaller than a pea

COLOR: Iron-black

OCCURRENCE: Very common

NOTES: Only a handful of minerals in Washington and Oregon will be attracted to a magnet, and magnetite is the most abundant of them. An iron-bearing mineral, magnetite always exhibits a metallic black coloration, though it is typically not as brightly lustrous as other similarly colored minerals. Well-formed magnetite crystals are octahedral (eight-faced) and resemble two four-sided pyramids placed base to base. When crystals are present, identification is simple thanks to their shape and magnetism. Unfortunately, like many minerals, crystals are quite rare and magnetite is far more common as nondescript grains or masses embedded in rocks. It is an important constituent of many rocks, particularly in igneous rocks, such as basalt. When those rocks weather, magnetite grains are freed and concentrate in sand and gravel. Magnetite grains are so prevalent that passing a magnet over a sandy river bank, for example, will yield many small examples. Visually, magnetite can be easily confused with hematite (page 145) and ilmenite (page 149), but hematite isn't magnetic and ilmenite is only weakly so.

WHERE TO LOOK: Dragging a magnet through gravel or sand will net you magnetite grains virtually anywhere in Washington or Oregon, particularly in rivers. Crystals, though tiny, have been found in the area around Portland, Oregon.

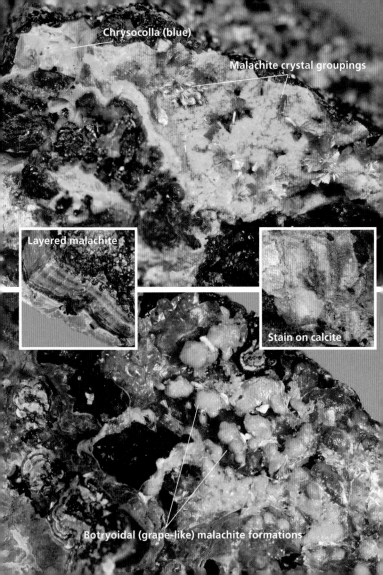

Chrysocolla (blue)

Malachite crystal groupings

Layered malachite

Stain on calcite

Botryoidal (grape-like) malachite formations

Malachite

HARDNESS: 3.5–4 **STREAK:** Light green

Occurrence

ENVIRONMENT: Mountains, road cuts, quarries

WHAT TO LOOK FOR: Soft green crusts or masses, often with a distinctly fibrous appearance and a banded cross section

SIZE: Specimens of malachite are often smaller than a pea

COLOR: Light to dark green

OCCURRENCE: Rare

NOTES: Malachite is a colorful and very popular collectible mineral. Like chrysocolla (page 99), malachite forms primarily when copper-bearing minerals weather and decompose. Malachite develops in a wide variety of geological environments, and it is found in everything from basalt to granite to serpentine, but it always occurs in various shades of green. If crystals are present, they typically take the form of delicate needles, with crystals often arranged into bundles or fan-shaped groupings, though massive specimens are more common. Masses often take the form of crude crusts or dusty coatings atop other minerals or embedded within rocks. Even when poorly formed, however, specimens typically exhibit a fibrous or silky cross section stemming from the tiny needle-like crystals that make up malachite. Crusts of malachite are also often layered, giving specimens a layered appearance when broken. Chrysocolla is the only mineral you're likely to confuse with malachite, though chrysocolla does not have any visible crystal structure, is typically softer, and easily dehydrates, becoming crumbly.

WHERE TO LOOK: Malachite can be found in small amounts in many places in Washington, including Denny Mountain in King County and dozens of localities in Stevens and Okanogan Counties. In Oregon, Wallowa and Harney Counties produce specimens from a wide variety of rocks.

171

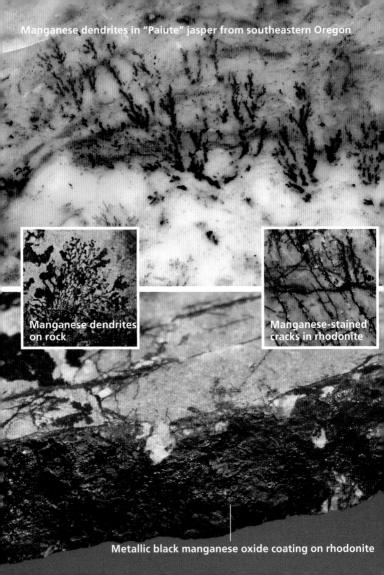

Manganese dendrites in "Paiute" jasper from southeastern Oregon

Manganese dendrites on rock

Manganese-stained cracks in rhodonite

Metallic black manganese oxide coating on rhodonite

Manganese oxides

HARDNESS: <6 **STREAK:** Black

Occurrence

ENVIRONMENT: Mountains, road cuts, quarries

WHAT TO LOOK FOR: Dusty black crusts or tree-like growths formed on the surfaces of rocks or minerals

SIZE: Coatings of manganese oxides can be any size, and many measure several inches across

COLOR: Gray to black, dark brown; often with a metallic sheen

OCCURRENCE: Uncommon

NOTES: Manganese is a common metallic element found in many Pacific Northwest minerals. In a process called oxidation, it is quick to bond with oxygen. Consequently, there are several oxides of manganese, all of which are notoriously difficult to identify thanks to their nearly identical appearances and hardnesses. Most appear as black crusts or coatings on other manganese-bearing minerals, such as rhodonite (page 217). When thick, these coatings can be fairly hard and even somewhat metallic, though most are very thin, dust-like and chalky. Though easily overlooked, these crusts of manganese oxides often "identify themselves" by leaving a black charcoal-like dust on your hands—a tell-tale sign of manganese. Since crystals of manganese oxide minerals are often nonexistent, these minerals are not sought after. Dendrites are the exception. They are unique plant-like mineral formations that formed within tiny cracks in rocks or other minerals. Dendrites typically consist of manganese oxides. They form when water deposits manganese on surfaces, so they are often found when breaking weathered rocks.

WHERE TO LOOK: The rhodonite found on and near Mount Higgins in Washington contains veins of black oxides, often with branching dendrites. In both states, carefully inspect broken surfaces of jaspers and rocks for dendrites.

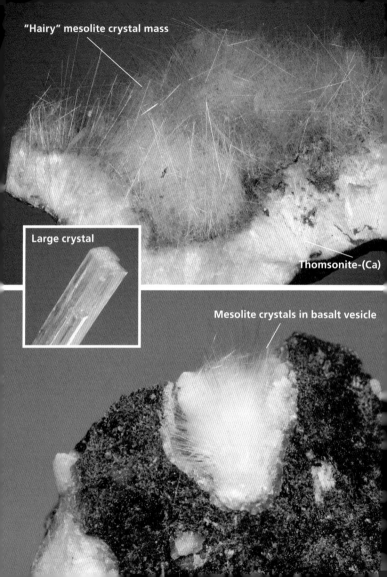

"Hairy" mesolite crystal mass

Large crystal

Thomsonite-(Ca)

Mesolite crystals in basalt vesicle

Mesolite

HARDNESS: 5 **STREAK:** White

Occurrence

ENVIRONMENT: Rivers, quarries, road cuts

WHAT TO LOOK FOR: Very fine, delicate, needle-like crystals arranged into spray- or fan-shaped aggregates within basalt

SIZE: Individual crystals are very thin, sometimes not much thicker than a hair, but can be up to an inch long

COLOR: Colorless to white or cream-colored; rarely yellow

OCCURRENCE: Uncommon

NOTES: There are over a dozen zeolites found in Washington and Oregon, and mesolite is a spectacular example. The zeolites are a group of complex minerals that form in vesicles (gas bubbles) in basalt as it is affected by alkaline water. Because there is a large amount of basalt in the region, zeolites are prominent collectibles. Like thomsonite-(Ca) (page 241) and natrolite (page 185), mesolite forms extremely delicate needle-like crystals that occasionally occur alone but are often arranged into radial fan- or spray-shaped groupings. Since thomsonite-(Ca) and natrolite form in the same way, identifying mesolite can be difficult. Unfortunately, a hardness test doesn't help, as all three minerals have nearly the same hardness. You therefore have to rely on crystal shape to identify mesolite. When the crystals are coarse enough, mesolite's crystals show a square cross section while thomsonite-(Ca)'s are flatter and more blade-like. Natrolite's crystals are square, too, but mesolite's crystals are typically much finer, sometimes no thicker than a hair, and are more flexible.

WHERE TO LOOK: In Washington, the basalt near Skookumchuck Dam in Bucoda has produced coarse, museum-quality specimens. In Oregon, basalt in Goble is lucrative as are many basalt outcrops in Grant County, particularly near Ritter.

Muscovite mica (shiny gray) in granodiorite

Rare iron-stained phlogopite crystals ($\frac{1}{64}$")

Crude mica crystals in granite

Feathery grouping of muscovite crystals in feldspar

Mica group

HARDNESS: 2.5–3 **STREAK:** Colorless

Occurrence

ENVIRONMENT: All environments

WHAT TO LOOK FOR: Shiny, often dark-colored minerals that occur in thin, flexible sheet-like crystals that almost appear metallic

SIZE: Micas occur in crystals that are very thin but up to several inches wide; most samples are smaller than an inch

COLOR: Gray to brown, yellow to green, black

OCCURRENCE: Very common

NOTES: The micas are a large group of closely related minerals that share a unique set of traits. Several micas are found throughout the Pacific Northwest—phlogopite, muscovite, celadonite, biotite, and the rare polylithionite, to name a few. All micas form as thin sheet-like crystals that are often hexagonal (six-sided) in shape and grow in layered stacks called books. These growths really resemble a book; in many specimens, individual crystals are so flexible that they can be torn out like a book's pages. This trait, along with its low hardness, makes mica easy to identify when crystallized. But micas are also rock-builders (minerals primarily found as components of rocks). You're much more likely to find mica as masses embedded in rock, especially granite and schist. In most rocks, micas are easy to identify as dark, soft flakes that are often very lustrous, sometimes almost metallic. In metamorphic rocks like schist, micas often give the rocks a "glittery" look. Celadonite (page 87) is the primary exception, as it forms microscopic crystals.

WHERE TO LOOK: Celadonite is common almost anywhere there is basalt, but nice specimens are found along the Clackamas River in Oregon. Muscovite crystals can rarely be found near Riverside, Washington, and phlogopite crystals can be found in andesite at Summit Rock in Klamath County, Oregon.

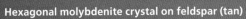

Hexagonal molybdenite crystal on feldspar (tan)

Molybdenite

HARDNESS: 1–1.5 **STREAK:** Grayish green to black

Occurrence

ENVIRONMENT: Mountains, road cuts, quarries

WHAT TO LOOK FOR: Small, very soft, very shiny metallic six-sided crystals, or flakes, veins or masses embedded in rock

SIZE: Molybdenite crystals are rarely larger than your thumbnail, while masses and veins can measure a few inches

COLOR: Metallic gray, bluish-gray

OCCURRENCE: Rare

NOTES: Metallic minerals often share so many similarities that identifying them can be a headache. But that is not the case with molybdenite. Unlike nearly every other metallic mineral in the Pacific Northwest, molybdenite is extremely soft and you can easily scratch it with your fingernails. Thin specimens are even surprisingly flexible. Thanks to its low hardness and its distinctive shade of brightly lustrous gray (sometimes with a bluish tint), identifying molybdenite is generally quite simple. Well-crystallized specimens have a hexagonal, or six-sided, shape, and are very thin and leaf-like, typically intergrown into layered stacks with tapered or blade-like edges. Crystals are quite rare, however, and veins or flakes in rocks like granite are more common. If you confuse another mineral for molybdenite, it will likely be a mica (page 177), as many of the different mica minerals crystallize in a similar manner and are so brightly lustrous they look almost metallic. The key difference between them is that the micas are far more abundant and present in nearly every rock environment. In addition, molybdenite has two streaks: grayish green on a streak plate and black on paper.

WHERE TO LOOK: The best molybdenite crystals have come from private mines in Chelan County, Washington. Specimens can also be found in granite in Grant County, Oregon.

179

"Hairy" mordenite crystals coating a calcite crystal

Heulandite-(Ca) crystal

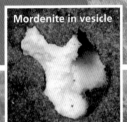

Mordenite in vesicle

Mordenite "ball"

Mordenite (white) on clinoptilolite in a thunder egg geode

Same specimen as left photo under short-wave ultraviolet light

Mordenite

HARDNESS: 3–4 **STREAK:** White

Occurrence

ENVIRONMENT: Rivers, quarries, road cuts

WHAT TO LOOK FOR: Very fine, delicate, hair-like crystals intergrown into fibrous "mats" or "sprays" within basalt

SIZE: Individual mordenite crystals are rarely more than an inch long, but intergrowths can measure up to several inches

COLOR: Colorless to white; pale pink or pale yellow uncommon

OCCURRENCE: Uncommon

NOTES: When volcanic rock is affected by groundwater, mineral molecules accumulate in the rock's vesicles, or gas bubbles, leading to the formation of new minerals. This is how the zeolite group of minerals form; mordernite is one of well over a dozen zeolites found in Washington and Oregon. Unfortunately, due to several similar-looking zeolites, mordernite can be often difficult to identify. Mordenite is almost always white in color and forms as extremely fine, delicate needle-like crystals that are often as thin as hair. These crystals are always intergrown with many others and are often arranged into radial groupings, creating fibrous, silky "sprays." Occasionally these formations are so complete that they form ball-like structures. No matter what form it takes, mordenite nearly always has a "fuzzy" look. Mordenite is generally found in vesicles alongside other zeolites, particularly heulandite-(Ca) (page 147), but you're most likely to confuse it with thomsonite-(Ca) (page 241) and mesolite (page 175). Those zeolites, however, form coarser crystals more often, whereas mordenite's are always very fine and are occasionally fluorescent in ultraviolet light.

WHERE TO LOOK: Basalt along Rock Creek, near Stevenson, Washington, produces beautiful specimens. Basalt quarries in Polk County, Oregon, particularly near Dallas, are great, too.

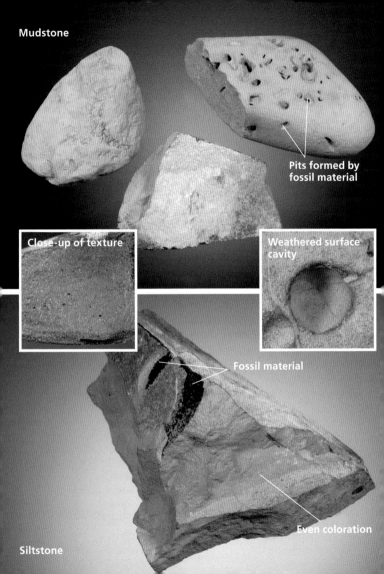

Mudstone

Pits formed by
fossil material

Close-up of texture

Weathered surface
cavity

Fossil material

Even coloration

Siltstone

Mudstone/Siltstone

HARDNESS: N/A **STREAK:** N/A

Occurrence

ENVIRONMENT: Fields, road cuts, quarries

WHAT TO LOOK FOR: Soft dense rocks easily scratched by a knife and consisting of very tiny grains, resembling hard clay

SIZE: Mudstone and siltstone are rocks that occur in large masses and specimens can be found in any size

COLOR: Light to dark gray, tan to brown, occasionally reddish

OCCURRENCE: Common

NOTES: Mudstone and siltstone are two sedimentary rocks that are identified by the size of the mineral grains within them. Most sedimentary rocks are visually identified this way—sandstone, for example, consists of sand-sized particles no larger than $1/12$ of an inch. The grains in mudstone and siltstone are microscopic, around $1/5{,}000$ of an inch in siltstone and as small as $1/12{,}500$ of an inch in mudstone. The individual grains consist of a combination of weathered minerals and clay particles that formed when feldspar decomposed (page 123). But because their individual grains are so tiny, distinguishing mudstone from siltstone is nearly impossible, as it requires an extremely strong microscope. For all intents and purposes, this is impossible for the amateur; it's also not necessary, as both rocks are easy to differentiate from other rock types. Both rocks formed on the lake or ocean bottom, both occur in large beds, and they each have a slightly gritty feel with even, consistent coloration and no layering. Layered mudstone is actually shale (page 227).

WHERE TO LOOK: Mudstone can be seen along U.S. 199 southwest of Grants Pass, Oregon, as well as along the Oregon coast, particularly near Arch Cape. In Washington, the northern end of Puget Sound contains mudstone and siltstone, particularly around Bellingham and Sedro Woolley.

Large specimen with multiple radial "sprays" of natrolite crystals

Coarse crystals

Radial grouping

Needle-like crystals

High-quality natrolite specimen

Natrolite

HARDNESS: 5–5.5 **STREAK:** White

Occurrence

ENVIRONMENT: Rivers, road cuts, quarries

WHAT TO LOOK FOR: Delicate, brittle needle-like crystals arranged into radial "puff balls" within vesicles (gas bubbles) in basalt

SIZE: Individual crystals are typically no more than a half inch long; crystal groupings can measure up to several inches

COLOR: Colorless to white, cream-colored to yellow or brownish

OCCURRENCE: Uncommon

NOTES: A close mineralogical cousin to mesolite (page 175) and scolecite (page 223), natrolite is another of Washington and Oregon's many zeolite minerals. The zeolites form within vesicles (gas bubbles) in basalt. As the rock is affected by alkaline groundwater, chemical compounds are trapped in the rock's cavities and accumulate, contributing to the formation of minerals such as chlorite, clay and zeolites. Natrolite is one of the most iconic zeolites, and it is widely collected around the world. It forms as delicate, often colorless, needle-like crystals that exhibit a square cross section when viewed on end. Unfortunately, this description matches mesolite and scolecite, two other zeolites, and sometimes they cannot be conclusively identified without a lab. But there are a few traits to look for that may help. All three of the aforementioned zeolites (among others) typically develop radial "sprays" of crystals, but natrolite's often extend in all directions, forming what appear to be "puff balls" of crystals. In addition, when comparing specimens of natrolite, scolecite and mesolite, natrolite's crystals will generally be the coarsest and most brittle.

WHERE TO LOOK: Vesicular basalt around Drain, Oregon, has produced many samples, and in Washington, basalt in the Doty Hills, southwest of Olympia, produces specimens.

185

Obsidian

Dull brown weathered surface

Conchoidal fracture

Backlit specimen showing translucence

Obsidian with brown coloration (often called "mahogany" obsidian)

Obsidian

HARDNESS: 6–7 **STREAK:** N/A

Occurrence

ENVIRONMENT: Mountains, quarries, road cuts

WHAT TO LOOK FOR: Dark, black, translucent rock that appears distinctly like glass

SIZE: Obsidian can be found in any size, from pebbles to boulders

COLOR: Black common; brown to green, gray uncommon

OCCURRENCE: Uncommon

NOTES: Obsidian is a rock—or is it a mineral? If you're simply looking at a specimen of obsidian, it can be hard to tell. The classification of obsidian has confused people for ages; technically, it is considered an igneous rock because of its complex (and varied) chemical composition. Yet obsidian is brightly lustrous and translucent and often has very even coloration, and it just doesn't look like any other type of rock. That's because obsidian is actually volcanic glass; it formed from molten rhyolite (page 219) and cooled before the minerals within could crystallize, instead hardening as a jumble of molecules. This can happen a few ways, but in the Pacific Northwest obsidian typically formed when highly viscous (thick, sticky) rhyolite lava rich with silica (quartz material), but almost devoid of water, cooled as a large mass. The extremely thick nature of the lava prevented mineral growth. As a type of natural glass, obsidian is unmistakable for any other rock. It has sharp edges when broken, exhibits conchoidal fracturing (when struck, circular cracks appear), and it is translucent in thin sections. Most obsidian is black, but it can contain "smears" of gray or brown. Finally, obsidian develops a dull, dusty surface coating when weathered, which can be broken away to reveal the glassy interior.

WHERE TO LOOK: Glass Butte is a mountain of obsidian located along US-20 about 80 miles southeast of Bend, Oregon.

Gabbro

Olivine grains (yellowish)

Olivine grains from beach sand

Polished masses of olivine

Olivine group

HARDNESS: 6.5–7 **STREAK:** Colorless

Occurrence

ENVIRONMENT: All environments

WHAT TO LOOK FOR: Very hard, glassy green masses, often as embedded grains or veins within rocks or loose in rivers

SIZE: Masses of olivine can be very large and measure in feet, but most specimens are fist-sized or smaller

COLOR: Yellow-green to dark green, gray-green, yellow to brown

OCCURRENCE: Common

NOTES: The olivine group consists primarily of two minerals, forsterite and fayalite. But due to their similar appearance and chemical makeup, telling them apart can be very difficult without a lab, so most specimens are just labelled "olivine" (though forsterite is far more common). Olivine is an important rock-building mineral and is most abundant as grains or masses embedded in dark volcanic rocks like basalt and gabbro. It is typically found in shades of yellowish green but turns a rusty brown color when highly weathered. Its characteristic color, combined with its high hardness, makes olivine fairly easy to identify, though there are a few minerals that you could confuse with it. Various feldspars (page 123) may look similar but are typically softer and often blocky in shape, even when embedded in rocks. Epidote (page 119) often shares a very similar green color, but is primarily found as striated (grooved) crystals whereas olivines are almost always massive. Finally, grains and pebbles of olivine are common in river gravel and sand.

WHERE TO LOOK: Perhaps the most spectacular "specimen" is the Twin Sisters Mountain near Bellingham, Washington, which is formed of dunite, a very rare rock consisting almost entirely of olivine. Collectible specimens are found in Skagit County, Washington, and Josephine County, Oregon.

189

Colored opals from Oregon

Cristobalite-filled vesicle

Colorless opal-A

Opal from Juniper Ridge, OR

Opal on rock from Opal Butte, OR

Opal

HARDNESS: 5.5–6.5 **STREAK:** White

Occurrence

ENVIRONMENT: Road cuts, quarries, fields

WHAT TO LOOK FOR: Smooth masses of light-colored material that greatly resemble glass, often within cavities or thunder eggs

SIZE: Masses of opal are typically smaller than your palm

COLOR: Colorless to white or gray is common; yellow to brown, blue, pink, or iridescent multicolored is less common

OCCURRENCE: Uncommon

NOTES: The name opal refers to several forms of silica, the same material that forms quartz (page 209). Unlike quartz, however, opal has no definite, organized internal crystal structure, and some varieties are even amorphous, which means that they have no internal structure at all and are essentially glass. Organized structure or not, all opals form massively and have little to no predetermined outward appearance. Instead, opals form as translucent glass blobs; these masses fill cavities in rock, becoming embedded in the host stone. Cristobalite is one of the most common forms of opal and is also the most internally organized, containing microscopic spheres of silica arranged into stacks. Called "common opal," cristobalite is typically opaque, white and often has a chalky texture. Other varieties, especially a type called opal-A, are more lustrous, more translucent, and more colorful than cristobalite. Opal-A is often found in shades of blue, pink, yellow, or is multicolored. This gemmy variety is the most sought after and can develop in botryoidal (grape-like) or rounded masses. Due to opal's massive nature, hardness, and glass-like features, it's fairly easy to identify.

WHERE TO LOOK: Opal Butte, in Morrow County, Oregon, has produced many incredible specimens. In Washington, weathered basalt around Spokane has yielded specimens.

Petrified wood

Preserved wood grain

Growth rings

Detail of pores

Petrified wood from ocean beach

Preserved bark features

Polished petrified wood

Petrified wood

HARDNESS: N/A **STREAK:** N/A

Occurrence

ENVIRONMENT: Shorelines, rivers, fields, quarries

WHAT TO LOOK FOR: Hard masses of material with features resembling wood grain, pores, tree rings, or tree bark

SIZE: Samples of petrified wood are often fist-sized or smaller but can be as large as a modern-day log or tree

COLOR: Varies greatly, often multicolored and banded; commonly white to gray, tan to yellow, or brown to black

OCCURRENCE: Rare

NOTES: Petrified wood is what rock collectors call fossilized wood. But unlike most fossilized plants, which are often very brittle and delicate, petrified wood typically consists of jasper (page 153), chalcedony (page 91), or opal (page 191), making specimens hard, weather resistant, and often very colorful. The wood is often so well preserved that growth rings and layers are present, and specimens sometimes contain bark and even branches, making for beautiful and interesting specimens. But despite petrified wood's unique appearance, it can be difficult to identify, especially when one finds a small fragment. Jasper and chalcedony are far more common, and many specimens of those materials can be banded or layered. To determine if your specimen is fossilized wood, look for other telltale signs, such as circular pore-like structures or surfaces that resemble tree bark. A piece of petrified wood can also resemble agate (page 47), but agates are rounder and normally more translucent.

WHERE TO LOOK: Beaches near Bandon, Oregon, often produce specimens, including rare petrified palm wood. The Deschutes area, near Bend, also produces specimens. In Washington, the area around Saddle Mountain and Yakima Canyon are famous for petrified wood.

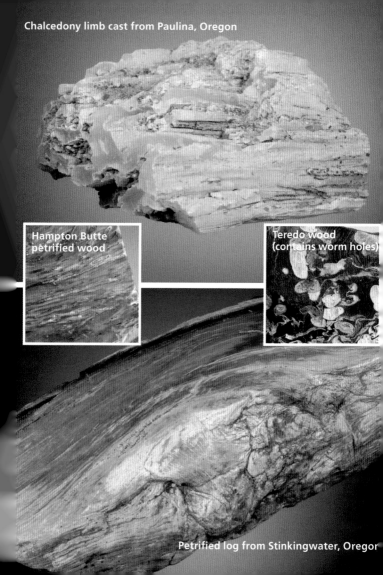

Chalcedony limb cast from Paulina, Oregon

Hampton Butte petrified wood

Teredo wood (contains worm holes)

Petrified log from Stinkingwater, Oregon

Petrified wood, varieties

HARDNESS: N/A **STREAK:** N/A

Occurrence

ENVIRONMENT: Shorelines, rivers, fields, quarries

WHAT TO LOOK FOR: Hard masses of material with features resembling wood grain, pores, tree rings, or tree bark

SIZE: Samples of petrified wood are often fist-sized or smaller but can be as large as a modern-day log or tree

COLOR: Varies greatly, often multicolored and banded; white to gray, tan to yellow or brown, green

OCCURRENCE: Very rare

NOTES: Like the Pacific Northwest's agates and jaspers, collectors have named specific types of petrified wood after their discoverers and the localities where they are found. And while these names rarely denote any kind of mineralogical differences, they do often signify exactly where specimens originated. "Stinkingwater petrified wood," for example, is known for its very well-preserved bark and wood grain and is found in the area around Stinkingwater, Oregon. Petrified wood from Hampton Butte, Oregon, is known for its green hues, possibly caused by the inclusion of copper minerals, and it is one of the most collectible varieties. But the specimens from near Paulina and Post, Oregon, are perhaps the most exciting. Specimens from this area are "limb casts," which formed when molten lava encased a tree, forming a tree-shaped cavity that later filled with gray chalcedony (page 91). Finally, many petrified woods are frequently called "agatized wood," but this isn't technically accurate. They actually consist of jasper (or rarely chalcedony), and the agate-like banding is preserved growth rings.

WHERE TO LOOK: Chalcedony limb casts are found in the areas around Paulina and Post in Oregon, while green petrified wood comes from Hampton Butte, Oregon.

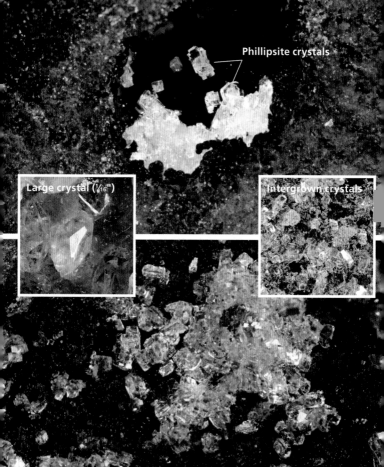

Basalt vesicle (about ⅛" across) lined with black clay

Phillipsite crystals

Large crystal (¹⁄₁₆")

Intergrown crystals

Tiny phillipsite crystals (most less than ³⁄₆₄") on black clay

Phillipsite

HARDNESS: 4–4.5 **STREAK:** White

Occurrence

ENVIRONMENT: Road cuts, quarries

WHAT TO LOOK FOR: Tiny, colorless, glassy rectangular crystals tipped with a four-sided point found within cavities in basalt

SIZE: Individual phillipsite crystals are rarely larger than ⅛ inch

COLOR: Colorless to white; rarely yellow to orange or red

OCCURRENCE: Rare

NOTES: Like chabazite-(Ca) (page 89) or natrolite (page 185), phillipsite is another of the Pacific Northwest's many zeolites. The zeolite group consists of minerals that form within cavities in rock affected by alkaline groundwater. Zeolites often form within vesicles (gas bubbles) in basalt. There are three chemically distinct but visually identical forms of phillipsite in Washington and Oregon—varieties rich in potassium, calcium or sodium. Without lab identification, however, there is no way to differentiate them, so specimens are often just labeled as phillipsite. Phillipsite forms as tiny elongated crystals that are generally rectangular in shape with small tapered points at each end. Crystals often have a square cross section, and whole well-formed crystals exhibit a four-sided point when viewed on end. While magnification is nearly always required to see these traits, this shape is quite distinctive and important to note. While phillipsite crystals are often quite elongated, they are not nearly as thin and delicate as the hair-like crystals of other zeolites (such as natrolite); this may also help you identify it. Finally, phillipsite is very often twinned, or exhibits two or more crystals intergrown through each other, which may help identify a specimen.

WHERE TO LOOK: Basalt road cuts in several locations in Grant County, Oregon, produce specimens. In Washington, try basalt in the area around Kalama, near the Columbia River.

Beach-worn porphyry with light-colored feldspar crystals

Detail of feldspar crystals

Hornblende crystal in porphyry

Andesite porphyry

Basalt porphyry

Porphyry

HARDNESS: N/A **STREAK:** N/A

Occurrence

ENVIRONMENT: All environments

WHAT TO LOOK FOR: Rocks with large, easily visible crystals embedded in a darker, fine-grained material

SIZE: Porphyry is found in any size, from pebbles to mountains

COLOR: Varies greatly; gray to black or brown with mottled spots of white to gray, yellow to orange, or pink

OCCURRENCE: Common

NOTES: Porphyry is a unique type of rock because it contains two distinct textures. Because they consist of mineral grains with a consistent size, most rocks have a uniform texture and appearance. Granite, for example, forms when magma (molten rock) cools deep within the earth, allowing the crystals within it to grow large enough to become visible. This gives granite its mottled, coarse texture. Unlike granite, basalt cools very quickly on or near the earth's surface, and it has a very fine, dense appearance with nearly microscopic mineral grains. Porphyry cooled at two different stages, giving it a combination of both textures. Like granite, it exhibits large crystals, but they are embedded in a dense, fine-grained base. In most varieties of porphyry, the conspicuous blocky or elongated crystals are feldspars (page 123) embedded in basalt (page 83). This is called porphyritic basalt, or basalt porphyry. Andesite (page 71) is very frequently porphyritic as well, and this is one of the rock's key identifying features. Though porphyry is easy to identify visually, be careful not to confuse poorly formed crystals with vesicles (gas bubbles) in rock, which will be round and often hollow.

WHERE TO LOOK: Specimens of porphyry are easily found anywhere along Oregon's Pacific Coast. Andesite is common in the area around Mount Baker in northwestern Washington.

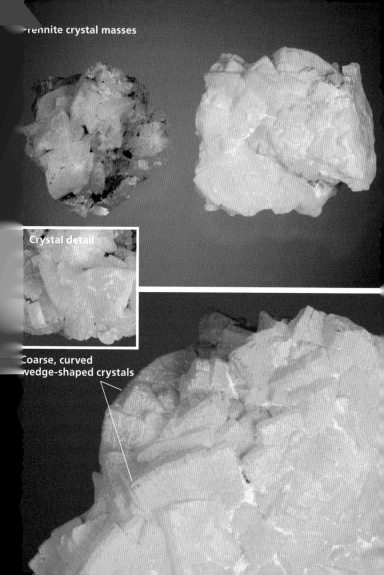

Prennite crystal masses

Crystal detail

Coarse, curved
wedge-shaped crystals

Prehnite

HARDNESS: 6–6.5 **STREAK:** White

Occurrence

ENVIRONMENT: Quarries, road cuts, rivers

WHAT TO LOOK FOR: White or pale green crusts and masses of intergrown hard, curving, wedge-like crystal groupings

SIZE: Individual crystals are thumbnail-sized or smaller while masses can measure several inches or more

COLOR: White to gray, pale green to yellow, brown

OCCURRENCE: Rare

NOTES: From igneous to metamorphic rocks, prehnite can form in several different geological environments. Yet despite the abundance of these types of rocks in Washington and Oregon, prehnite is a surprisingly rare mineral in the region. Much like datolite (page 115), prehnite can form in cavities within volcanic rocks, particularly basalt or andesite, as the rocks are affected by mineral-rich groundwater. But, like garnet (page 133), prehnite can also form as a result of metamorphic activity changing and altering rock; prehnite can form when molten rock rises and contacts limestone. When this happens, prehnite crystals can grow large enough that their shape and other characteristics are easy to observe, and this can aid in identification. Crystals typically appear as intergrown clusters of slightly curved wedge- or blade-like crystals, often with blocky or step-like edges. This shape is normally enough to distinguish prehnite from datolite, but datolite is also softer. Prehnite can also form botryoidally (in grape-like clusters); such formations may look like chalcedony (page 91), but chalcedony is harder.

WHERE TO LOOK: The area around Vesper Peak in Snohomish County, Washington, is known for large crystals in meta-morphic rocks, while Wallowa County in Oregon produces specimens formed within cavities in basalt and andesite.

201

Ankerite crystals

Irregular pyrite mass

Large pyrite crystal

Pyritohedron

Pyrite vein in agate

Striations (grooves)

Cubic pyrite crystals

Pyrite

HARDNESS: 6–6.5 **STREAK:** Greenish gray

Occurrence

ENVIRONMENT: Mountains, rivers, quarries, fields, road cuts

WHAT TO LOOK FOR: Common, brittle, metallic brassy yellow mineral often found in cubic shapes and embedded in rock

SIZE: Pyrite crystals are generally thumbnail-sized and smaller, but can occasionally grow to fist-sized or larger

COLOR: Brassy yellow to metallic brown

OCCURRENCE: Common

NOTES: Pyrite, often called "fool's gold" by amateurs due to its gold-like color, is one of the most common collectible minerals. Found in dozens of geological environments, pyrite consists of iron and sulfur. When it crystallizes, it forms either as a cube with striated (grooved) faces, or as a pyritohedron, a shape that consists of twelve pentagonal (five-sided) faces. Unfortunately, poorly formed masses of pyrite are most common. When found, pyrite is typically embedded within rocks and is difficult to separate, though the finest crystals form in cavities in igneous rocks, often alongside quartz. Whether it forms in massive chunks or well-crystallized cubes or pyritohedrons, identifying pyrite is easy. Its abundance means that any brassy yellow mineral can be assumed to be pyrite until other tests indicate otherwise. It's also harder than chalcopyrite (page 93), the mineral you're most likely to confuse it with, and it is not magnetic like cubanite (page 111). Finally, marcasite, a close cousin to pyrite, is similar in hardness, but it is rarer, doesn't form in cubes, and is more gray.

WHERE TO LOOK: Multiple mountainous locations in King County, Washington, have produced great crystals. In Oregon, many road cuts along the Clackamas River produce specimens.

Loose augite crystal

Augite (black) in gabbro

Hedenbergite crystals

Enstatite (1/16" tall)

Hedenbergite mass on skarn

Pyroxene group

HARDNESS: 5–6.5 **STREAK:** Gray-green to white

Occurrence

ENVIRONMENT: All environments

WHAT TO LOOK FOR: Hard, dark, glassy masses embedded within coarse-grained rocks; black, blocky, sometimes fibrous crystals found within cavities in rocks, particularly within skarn

SIZE: Most pyroxenes occur in masses smaller than a thumbnail

COLOR: Dark brown to black, dark to light green, yellow

OCCURRENCE: Very common

NOTES: Closely related to the amphibole group (page 67), the pyroxenes are a family of rock-builders and are very common constituents of dark igneous rocks, particularly basalt and gabbro. As a large mineral group, there are several pyroxenes present in the Pacific Northwest, including augite, jadeite, hedenbergite, diopside, aegirine, and enstatite. Of these, augite is the most common, and it is discussed separately on page 79. Most pyroxenes crystallize in blocky, angular shapes and grow within cavities in rock or are found embedded in many different rock types, such as andesite and various metamorphic rocks. They are generally dark colored, and occur in shades of brown, black, green or yellow and are often very glassy in appearance. But most pyroxenes form as nondescript masses embedded in rock. To identify these specimens, look for signs of cleavage. When pyroxenes cleave (break) along their crystal structure, they do so at nearly ninety-degree angles, making blocky, step-like breaks. You don't have to break your specimens to see this; most specimens show some breakage naturally.

WHERE TO LOOK: The Vesper Peak area in Snohomish County, Washington, produces fantastic hedenbergite specimens in metamorphic rocks. Summit Rock in Klamath County, Oregon, yields fine enstatite crystals in andesite.

Crude hexagonal pyrrhotite crystal

Layered pyrrhotite crystals viewed on-edge

Pyrrhotite

HARDNESS: 3.5–4.5 **STREAK:** Dark gray to black

Occurrence

ENVIRONMENT: Mountains, quarries, road cuts

WHAT TO LOOK FOR: Thin, plate-like, six-sided crystals or irregular masses that are bronze-colored and magnetic

SIZE: Crystals are generally smaller than a thumbnail while masses can be up to several inches

COLOR: Bronze brown to brassy yellow, often with dark brown surface tarnish

OCCURRENCE: Rare

NOTES: Pyrrhotite is a particularly unique mineral in that it has a natural "flaw" within its crystal structure. Pyrrhotite is iron sulfide, a combination of iron and sulfur. As such, it is a close relative to pyrite (page 203), which has the same chemical composition. Pyrrhotite differs, however, because its crystal structure lacks some iron atoms, and there are voids in their place, creating uneven chemical bonds. This iron deficiency makes pyrrhotite magnetic, making it easier for collectors to identify it. Pyrite, which shares pyrrhotite's metallic yellow-brown coloration, is not magnetic. Chalcopyrite (page 93) and cubanite (page 111) are also very similar in composition and appearance, but chalcopyrite is not magnetic, either. Cubanite, on the other hand, is magnetic, but is far rarer than pyrrhotite and is often shinier in appearance; pyrrhotite is often darker. Finally, pyrrhotite is typically found as embedded masses, but crystals that resemble flat hexagons can occasionally be found, though these are actually two intersecting crystals.

WHERE TO LOOK: Pyrrhotite is very widespread in small amounts in Josephine County, Oregon, embedded in diabase and metamorphic rocks. In Washington, crystals can rarely be found in Snohomish County in metamorphic rocks.

Quartz crystal cluster

Quartz-filled vesicle

Quartz druse

Water-worn quartz
with mineral inclusions

Rough quartz mass

Water-worn
quartz

Quartz crystals

Granular quartz mass

Quartz

HARDNESS: 7 **STREAK:** White

Occurrence

ENVIRONMENT: All environments

WHAT TO LOOK FOR: Light-colored, translucent, glassy and very hard six-sided crystals, masses or veins in rock, or abundant white water-worn pebbles on beaches

SIZE: Quartz crystals can range from pinhead-sized points to crystals several inches long; masses can be any size

COLOR: Colorless to white when pure; frequently stained yellow to brown or red, and rarely purple

OCCURRENCE: Very common

NOTES: Twelve percent of the material in the earth's crust consists of quartz, and it is the most abundant mineral on earth. It's therefore essential for rock hounds to be familiar with it. Quartz consists of silica, the silicon- and oxygen-bearing compound that contributes to the formation of hundreds of minerals. It's found most often as uninteresting white masses in rocks such as granite, or as microscopic grains in chert (page 95). But collectors want crystals, and luckily, crystals are quite common too. They occur most often in rock cavities and take the form of elongated hexagonal (six-sided) prisms that terminate (end) in a point. Crystals are often intergrown with each other, sometimes as a thin crust of countless tiny crystals called druse. Until you recognize quartz's appearance, you can distinguish it from similar-looking minerals, such as calcite (page 85), by a hardness test. Quartz is harder than anything you'll easily find and won't be scratched by a knife. Its conchoidal fracture (when struck, circular cracks appear) is also distinct.

WHERE TO LOOK: Some of the finest crystals come from locations in King County, Washington. Lesser, water-worn specimens can be found all along the Pacific Coast in both states.

Smoky quartz crystal

Feldspar

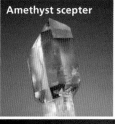

Amethyst scepter

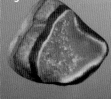

Agate

Phantom quartz crystal

Phantom

Quartz, varieties

HARDNESS: 7 **STREAK:** White

Occurrence

ENVIRONMENT: Mountains, road cuts, quarries

WHAT TO LOOK FOR: Translucent, gray or purple, glassy and very hard six-sided crystals or masses in rock

SIZE: Quartz crystals can range from pinhead-sized points to crystals several inches long; masses can be any size

COLOR: Varies by variety; brown to red, yellow to green, purple

OCCURRENCE: Uncommon to rare

NOTES: Quartz is so abundant that it forms in virtually every geological environment, resulting in many different varieties. Some varieties, like agates (page 47) or chert (page 95), are microcrystalline and formed when microscopic quartz crystals grow in masses. Other varieties, such as color variants, result from the inclusion of impurities within a crystal's structure. Amethyst, for example, is the famous purple variety of quartz; its unique coloration is caused by the irradiation of iron and aluminum impurities. Similarly, smoky quartz, the gray or black color variant of quartz, is caused by natural radiation interacting with aluminum impurities alone. Still other varieties of quartz are derived from unique structural modifications. Scepter crystals, for example, exhibit a wide crystal tip on the end of a narrower base. Phantoms are one of the more exciting structural variations of quartz. Samples of phantom quartz appear to have a second termination (a pointed tip) encased within the crystal. This is caused by two distinct periods of growth. These unique varieties of quartz can be fairly rare, however.

WHERE TO LOOK: Amethyst is often found in the area around Denny Mountain in Washington and Shellrock Mountain in Oregon. Smoky quartz can be found at Washington Pass in Okanogan County, Washington.

211

Beach-worn quartzite

Broken pebble

Grainy texture

Fairly pure quarzite

Layered quartzite

Quartzite

HARDNESS: ~7 **STREAK:** N/A

Occurrence

ENVIRONMENT: All environments

WHAT TO LOOK FOR: Very hard, grainy, light-colored rock that shares many of the same traits as quartz

SIZE: Quartzite can occur in any size, from pebbles to boulders

COLOR: White to gray, yellow to brown, red, often multicolored

OCCURRENCE: Common

NOTES: Sand consists mostly of quartz (page 209), and when sand accumulates and is compressed and cemented together, it forms sandstone (page 221). When sandstone is subsequently compressed, often in the presence of heat, the grains of sand fuse and the rock is metamorphosed into quartzite. As its name suggests, quartzite consists almost entirely of quartz, though it also includes minor amounts of clay minerals and calcite. Quartzite is an extremely hard, tough, and weather-resistant rock, and it is often found on beaches as rounded stones. It is typically light-colored; it is white when pure, but is also often yellow, brown, red, or even banded when stained by other minerals. Telling quartzite apart from other rocks can be difficult, but its consistent high hardness will help. Quartzite can greatly resemble chert (page 95), another quartz-based rock, and not surprisingly, quartzite is also similar to quartz, both in hardness and appearance. But chert is typically very opaque whereas quartzite will be translucent, and masses of quartz do not share quartzite's grainy or flaky texture.

WHERE TO LOOK: Quartzite can be found in eastern Washington, along the Idaho border, especially around Spokane. Large parts of central Oregon, particularly east of Paulina, as well as in the Wallowa Mountains, yield water-worn pebbles of quartzite, transported there by an ancient flood.

Small (less than ⅛") realgar crystals on quartz

Large crystal fragment

Crystals on rock

Backlit slice of sagenitic agate containing realgar crystals

⚠ **Realgar**

HARDNESS: 1.5–2 **STREAK:** Orange to red

ENVIRONMENT: Rivers, road cuts, quarries

Occurrence

WHAT TO LOOK FOR: Slender, striated (grooved), elongated bright red or orange crystals, often on calcite or quartz

SIZE: Crystals tend to remain very slender and shorter than ½ inch in length, but can rarely grow larger and wider

COLOR: Deep red, orange-red

OCCURRENCE: Rare

NOTES: Like cinnabar (page 101), realgar is one of the Pacific Northwest's most colorful collectible minerals and also one of the most potentially dangerous. That's because realgar contains arsenic, a notoriously toxic element; in fact, realgar is one of the world's primary sources of the metal. The fact that arsenic was once widely used as a rodent poison should make any collector wary, but it shouldn't stop you from collecting this beautiful mineral. If you take precautions, realgar is safe to collect. Be sure to handle it with gloves, avoid inhaling its dust, and don't heat or ingest it. It typically forms as slender elongated needles with striated, or deeply grooved, sides. Other minerals may have a similar crystal shape, but none in the region share realgar's bright red coloration. Crystals are often found on or in calcite or quartz, and a unique discovery near Trent, Oregon, yields sagenitic agates (page 61) containing realgar crystals along with masses of pure arsenic. With any specimen of realgar, be sure to store it in a dark place, as overexposure to light, especially sunlight, will cause it to disintegrate into an orange or yellow dust called pararealgar, which is toxic.

WHERE TO LOOK: Virtually all the best crystals in the region come from King County, Washington. Chalcedony and agates containing realgar are found near Trent, Oregon.

215

Rhodonite (pink) with quartz (white) and manganese oxides (black)

White rhodonite

Manganese oxide surface coating

Manganese oxide veins

Cut rhodonite mass

Rhodonite

HARDNESS: 5.5–6.5 **STREAK:** Colorless

Occurrence

ENVIRONMENT: Shoreline, road cuts, rivers, mountains

WHAT TO LOOK FOR: Hard pink embedded veins or rounded stones with reflective patches, often with streaks of black

SIZE: Rhodonite occurs as masses fist-sized and smaller

COLOR: Dark to pale pink, flesh-colored, light gray; occasionally with black surface coating

OCCURRENCE: Uncommon

NOTES: As a uniquely pink-colored mineral, rhodonite is a popular Pacific Northwest collectible. Unlike most states, where rhodonite is typically only produced in mines, both Washington and Oregon have many scattered but easily accessed rhodonite localities. Rhodonite is a manganese-bearing mineral closely related to the pyroxene group (page 205), and it therefore is quite hard. In our region, it is never found crystallized and is always massive, most often forming as veins in metamorphic rocks or alongside serpentine (page 225) where its color makes it highly conspicuous and easy to spot. You could hammer it free from its host rock, but the easiest way to collect it is after it has been weathered free. In some locations, pebbles of rhodonite can even be found on riverbanks. Few minerals resemble pink rhodonite, though pale-colored specimens may resemble some feldspars (page 123). When wet or polished, however, rhodonite exhibits reflective patches or spots indicative of internal crystals. In addition, masses of rhodonite often exhibit black streaks of manganese oxides (page 173).

WHERE TO LOOK: Rhodonite can be found near Holland in Josephine County in Oregon as river-worn stones. In Washington, rivers, road cuts, and hillsides at Mount Higgins, near Darrington, have produced specimens.

Orbicular rhyolite

Banded rhyolite

Reddish beach-worn rhyolite

Rhyolite fragments

Close-up of texture

"Lily pad" rhyolite

Pumice

Rhyolite

HARDNESS: 6–6.5 **STREAK:** N/A

Occurrence

ENVIRONMENT: Shoreline, rivers, quarries, road cuts, mountains

WHAT TO LOOK FOR: Hard, dense, fine-grained light-colored rock, often exhibiting many gas bubbles or stripes of color

SIZE: Rhyolite can be found in any size, from pebbles to boulders

COLOR: White to gray, light to dark brown, green; often mottled

OCCURRENCE: Common

NOTES: The eruption of Mount St. Helens in 1980 is perhaps one of the most well known volcanic events in the past few decades. A snow-capped volcano south of Seattle, Washington, Mount St. Helens' violent, explosive eruption resulted from the buildup of molten rhyolite rich with steam and other gases. Rhyolite is an igneous rock that forms when lava, or molten rock, that is rich in quartz (page 209) and feldspar (page 123) is erupted onto the earth's surface where it cools very rapidly. This rapid cooling causes the minerals within the lava to quickly solidify, preventing them from growing to a large, visible size. This gives rhyolite its dense, fine-grained appearance. If rhyolite had instead cooled slowly, deep within the earth, it would have become granite (page 143). Because of its high quartz content, rhyolite is harder and much lighter in color than other similar fine-grained volcanic rocks, such as basalt (page 83). In addition, slightly larger glassy mineral grains are sometimes visible, further distinguishing rhyolite from other volcanic rocks. Some specimens contain numerous vesicles (gas bubbles) made from trapped gases or display faint stripes of color caused by the movement of flowing lava.

WHERE TO LOOK: Rhyolite can be found all along the Cascade Mountain Range as rough, light-colored boulders.

Sandstone

Fossil shell in water-worn sandstone

Wacke

Fossil clamshell within sandstone

Visible grains

Sandstone

HARDNESS: N/A **STREAK:** N/A

Occurrence

ENVIRONMENT: All environments

WHAT TO LOOK FOR: Rocks that occur in layers and have a rough, gritty texture and appear as if made of sand

SIZE: Sandstone can be found in any size, from pebbles to cliffs

COLOR: White to yellow or brown, occasionally orange to reddish

OCCURRENCE: Very common

NOTES: Sedimentary rocks are often named for the particles of sediment from which they're made. Case in point, sandstone is formed primarily of sand, a familiar type of sediment. Sand is technically defined as consisting of detrital particles (particles produced as rocks weather and erode); individual sand grains are no larger than $1/12$ of an inch. As sand settled into huge beds at the bottom of seas and lakes, it was compressed, and small amounts of clay, calcite, and other soft minerals formed between the grains of sand, cementing them together. This gives sandstone a rough, gritty feel and, depending on the amount of compression during formation, you can often separate individual grains of sand with your bare hands. Sandstone also occasionally exhibits layering. These traits make sandstone easier than most sedimentary rocks to identify. A particular variety of sandstone common in the region is known as wacke. Wacke is a poorly organized sandstone that consists of particles of varying sizes that settled during underwater avalanches that "mixed up" different sediments. Wacke is often very "dirty," contains lots of clay and iron oxides, and is quick to weather.

WHERE TO LOOK: Beautifully weathered sandstone cliffs can be found along the Pacific Coast in both states. More spectacular examples can be seen in Washington's Olympic Mountains, which are formed largely of sandstone.

221

Scolecite crystal cluster

Coarse intergrown needles

Close-up of crystals

Tiny (1/32") scolecite crystals in basalt vesicle

Scolecite

HARDNESS: 5–5.5 **STREAK:** White

Occurrence

ENVIRONMENT: Rivers, quarries, road cuts

WHAT TO LOOK FOR: Coarsely crystallized radial "sprays" of slender needle-like crystals within vesicles (gas bubbles) in basalt

SIZE: Individual crystals are quite thin but up to an inch long; radial aggregates can measure up to an inch in width

COLOR: Colorless to white; pink to yellow or brown uncommon

OCCURRENCE: Uncommon in Washington; rare in Oregon

NOTES: Scolecite is another of Washington and Oregon's many zeolites. The zeolites are a group of chemically complex, hydrous minerals that form within vesicles (gas bubbles) in basalt as the rock is affected by alkaline water. Scolecite forms in colorless or white long, slender, needle-like crystals that are typically arranged into radial aggregates, or "sprays." It can be difficult to differentiate from other minerals, such as the very closely related zeolites natrolite (page 185), mesolite (page 175), and Thomsonite-(Ca) (page 241). Since performing a hardness test is nearly impossible on such delicate crystals, you'll need magnification to carefully inspect their crystal shape. Thomsonite-(Ca)'s crystals are typically blade-like and flatter in shape than scolecite's, which instead have a square cross section. Natrolite and mesolite crystals are also square, but natrolite crystals are generally coarser and mesolite's are much finer and more flexible. Finally, the base of a scolecite "spray," where all the crystals converge, is often very compact, chalky and opaque while the tips of the crystals are more translucent.

WHERE TO LOOK: Vesicles in basalt at many localities in Cowlitz County, Washington, have yielded scolecite formations. In Oregon, there are far fewer locations, but specimens have been found within vesicles in basalt in Lane County.

Serpentine mass

Calcite vein (white)

Orange-brown
weathered exterior

Vivid green antigorite

Texture of
serpentinite

Serpentinite

Serpentine group

HARDNESS: 3–5 **STREAK:** White

Occurrence

ENVIRONMENT: Rivers, road cuts, fields, mountains, quarries

WHAT TO LOOK FOR: Green to yellow massive minerals with a distinctly "greasy" feel, often layered and embedded in rock

SIZE: Serpentine minerals form massively and can be found in any size, though most specimens are typically under a foot long

COLOR: Light to dark green, gray-green, yellow to brown

OCCURRENCE: Common

NOTES: The serpentines are a unique group of minerals common to the Pacific Northwest. There are several serpentines found in Washington and Oregon, including antigorite, lizardite and chrysotile. The serpentines formed when peridotite, an olivine-rich rock that is common beneath the earth's crust, but rare on the surface, underwent metamorphosis. Peridotite underlies the basalt sea floor of the Pacific Ocean; when great pressure metamorphoses it, it turns into huge layers of serpentine minerals. But serpentines are slippery; they even have a "greasy" feel (which is one of the key identifying traits), so when the ocean floor was subducted beneath tectonic plates (see page 8), some of the serpentine slipped upwards to the earth's surface. Most serpentine minerals are dark green, soft and easily scratched by a knife. Chrysotile is an exception; it is a form of asbestos (be sure to wear a mask while collecting it) and has a fibrous texture and appearance. Serpentinite is a variety of rock composed primarily of serpentine minerals and shares their traits.

WHERE TO LOOK: In Oregon, serpentine is common in Josephine County as well as near Myrtle Creek where I-5 crosses a large formation. In Washington, serpentine is common near Twin Sisters Mountain in Whatcom County.

Shale

Layers

Leaf fossil

Shale layers

Slate layers

Layers

Slate

Shale/Slate

HARDNESS: <5.5 **STREAK:** N/A

Occurrence

ENVIRONMENT: Mountains, rivers, road cuts, fields

WHAT TO LOOK FOR: Fairly soft, fine-grained rocks that occur in large sheet-like formations with easily separated layers

SIZE: Shale formations can measure miles in size; slate formations tend to be smaller and are measurable in feet

COLOR: Shale tan to brown, gray to black; slate gray to black

OCCURRENCE: Shale is common; slate is rare

NOTES: Shale is a common sedimentary rock that formed at the bottom of very still bodies of water, and it consists of compacted and solidified mud. Over time, microscopic particles of clay minerals, micas and quartz—the remains of weathered and decomposed rocks and minerals—settled into distinct layers. In most bodies of shale, these layers are loosely bonded and you can separate them with a blade or even with your hands. Shale is a soft rock and easy to scratch with a knife; thanks to its low hardness, its fine-grained texture and distinctive layering, identifying it is simple. And, because of shale's aquatic origins, separating its layers can be a lucrative activity: plant fossils, such as leaf imprints, can sometimes be found within the rock. If shale is subjected to heat or pressure, it undergoes metamorphosis and is compacted and hardened into slate. Confusing the two is unlikely. Slate is far less abundant, and it is harder, has much thinner layers, is darker in color, and does not soften when soaked in water as shale typically does.

WHERE TO LOOK: The Chuckanut Formation consists of fossil-bearing shale and is accessible at Chuckanut Mountain in Bellingham, Washington. In Oregon, the area around Roseburg has a large amount of shale.

Coral

Shell fossil in sandstone

Seashell fragments

Banded coloration

Oyster shell

Bore holes in a boulder on Oregon's Pacific Coast

Shells

HARDNESS: 3.5–4 **STREAK:** White

Occurrence

ENVIRONMENT: Shorelines

WHAT TO LOOK FOR: Coiled, flattened or curving organic structures with ridges, stripes or lines, found on ocean beaches

SIZE: Most shells are smaller than your palm

COLOR: Varies greatly; white to gray, yellow to orange, pink to purple, brown to black

OCCURRENCE: Very common

NOTES: It may initially seem odd to include shells in a book about rocks and minerals, but one must consider what shells are made of. Shells are the hard exoskeletons left behind by dead mollusks. The shells that countless beachcombers collect from the sandy shores of the Pacific Coast are actually made of aragonite (page 75), a mineral produced by snails, clams, mussels and corals. Whole shells, especially those that are coiled, are clearly organic and don't normally confuse rock hounds, but small fragments of certain shells may exhibit bands or stripes and resemble agates (page 47) or jasper (page 153). Shells, however, are much softer than those minerals. In addition, some shell-like structures, such as coral, can resemble volcanic rocks filled with vesicles (gas bubbles), or even petrified wood (page 193), but all shells will slowly effervesce (fizz) and dissolve in acids, such as vinegar. Volcanic rocks and petrified wood won't. One unique occurrence of shells is within sandstone. These specimens are actually fossils, trapped within the crumbly, grainy sedimentary rock. Finally, you may come across seaside boulders filled with uniform, tube-like holes. These are not vesicles—they are boreholes made by mollusks.

WHERE TO LOOK: The Pacific Coast of both Washington and Oregon will yield shells and other sea life.

Intergrown wedge-shaped siderite crystals (tan)

Sphalerite

Stack of thin crystals

Siderite (brown) on feldspar

Sphärosiderite in basalt vesicle (gas bubble)

Siderite

HARDNESS: 3.5–4 **STREAK:** White to yellow

Occurrence

ENVIRONMENT: Mountains, quarries, road cuts

WHAT TO LOOK FOR: Soft, brown, blocky or layered sheet-like crystals, or spheres, within cavities in rock

SIZE: Individual siderite crystals or spheres are typically smaller than an inch; masses can measure up to several inches

COLOR: Light to dark brown, reddish brown, rarely black

OCCURRENCE: Uncommon

NOTES: Siderite is a close mineral cousin to calcite (page 85) and both share many similarities. But unlike calcite, siderite is fairly uncommon, and recognizable crystals don't form often, so you're not likely to confuse them. Siderite can form in several geological environments, but it is more abundant in sedimentary areas, such as in northeastern Washington. Nondescript masses are most common, and crystals are somewhat rare. Siderite crystals can take several shapes; they can be found as rhombohedrons (a shape resembling a leaning cube), in sheet-like stacks and layers, in wedge shapes, or as round spheres. (Siderite crystals with round spheres are technically considered a separate variety called sphärosiderite.) To identify siderite, whether crystals are present or not, look for rhombohedral cleavage (when carefully broken, siderite breaks into rhombohedrons). Also, place a drop of vinegar on it, siderite will effervesce (fizz) slightly. Even though siderite is normally darker than most calcite, you could confuse them. Calcite, however, is slightly softer and effervesces in acids much more vigorously.

WHERE TO LOOK: Quarries near Mount Vernon in Skagit County, Washington, are known for small crystals. In Oregon, many road cuts along Highway 224, about 55 miles southeast of Portland, are known for many minerals, including siderite.

Skarn

Grossular garnet

Texture detail

Close-up of skarn with grossular garnet (orange) and diopside (green)

Skarn

HARDNESS: N/A **STREAK:** N/A

Occurrence

ENVIRONMENT: Mountains, quarries, road cuts

WHAT TO LOOK FOR: Coarse-grained rock typically exhibiting many colors, many pockets of large mineral formations, and many reflective surfaces, resulting in a "sparkling" appearance

SIZE: Skarn occurs in enormous masses

COLOR: Varies greatly; multicolored with green, red to brown, white to gray, black

OCCURRENCE: Uncommon

NOTES: Skarn is a metamorphic rock produced by contact metamorphism, which occurs when a body of magma (molten rock) contacts existing layers of rock. In skarn's case, a mass of molten granite rose through the earth and met limestone (page 165). Through a process called metasomatism, hot mineral-rich water originating from the magma dissolved the limestone, enriching it with minerals and redepositing it as skarn once the rock cooled. This creates a skarn zone, a division between granite and limestone formations that contains many collectible minerals. Skarn is generally coarse-grained and exhibits many streaks and variations in color because of the many minerals within it. For example, red-brown colorations come from garnets (page 133), and green is from actinolite (page 45). Skarn often displays a sparkling appearance due to the reflective crystal faces of these minerals. Large embedded masses of garnet or pockets containing glassy crystals of various minerals are abundant, making skarn easy to identify and widely sought after.

WHERE TO LOOK: Vesper Peak in Snohomish County, Washington, is one of the most famous garnet localities in the state. The Wallowa Mountains in northeastern Oregon contain many skarn formations that yield epidote and garnet specimens.

233

Stibnite crystals within quartz

Stibnite "spray"

Coarse stibnite crystals in quartz

⚠ Stibnite

Occurrence

HARDNESS: 2 **STREAK:** Metallic gray

ENVIRONMENT: Mountains, fields, road cuts, quarries

WHAT TO LOOK FOR: Soft, silver-gray streaks or elongated, needle-like crystals with striated (grooved) sides, often arranged into radial "spray"-like groupings and embedded in rock

SIZE: Most stibnite crystals are no more than an inch or two long and less than ¼ inch wide

COLOR: Metallic gray to bluish silver

OCCURRENCE: Rare

NOTES: Since antiquity, stibnite has been the primary source of antimony, an element once used by ancient Egyptians as a cosmetic and utilized today in lead alloys and super-strong acids. Primarily a hydrothermal mineral, stibnite forms when hot mineral-rich volcanic water rises from deep within the earth and collects in cavities where the dissolved minerals can accumulate and crystallize. Not surprisingly, stibnite is frequently found embedded within other minerals, such as calcite and quartz. Though there are many localities throughout the Pacific Northwest where stibnite has been found, it is always found in small quantities, making it quite a rare find. Stibnite typically appears as long slender needles of soft, dark metal, often with striated (grooved) faces arranged into radial, fan-like groupings. Its structure, color and hardness are distinctive, though amateurs could mistake embedded crystals of boulangerite (page 257) and molybdenite (page 179) for stibnite. Boulangerite is slightly harder, while molybdenite is softer and has a greenish streak. Wash your hands after handling, as antimony is toxic.

WHERE TO LOOK: King, Chelan and Ferry Counties in Washington have all produced stibnite from old mines and road cuts. In Oregon, Baker County has yielded the most specimens.

235

Stilbite (Ca) crystal mass

Wheat-sheaf cluster

Stilbite fragment

Well-formed stilbite crystal

Pearly surface luster

Stilbite-(Ca)

HARDNESS: 3.5–4 **STREAK:** White

Occurrence

ENVIRONMENT: Rivers, quarries, road cuts

WHAT TO LOOK FOR: Thin, pearly, light-colored crystals arranged into fan-shaped aggregates in vesicles (gas bubbles) in basalt

SIZE: Individual crystals are rarely larger than ¼ inch in length

COLOR: Colorless to white or pink when pure; when impure, commonly yellow to brown, gray, orange to red

OCCURRENCE: Uncommon

NOTES: Stilbite-(Ca) is a zeolite; the zeolites are a group of chemically complex hydrous minerals that form in vesicles (gas bubbles) in basalt as the rock is affected by water. Because basalt is so commonplace in Washington and Oregon, there are many zeolites present as well. Frustratingly, many zeolites can be seemingly indistinguishable from each other, but stilbite-(Ca) is an exception as it has several distinctive traits. And you'll need to know them, because stilbite-(Ca) is rarely found alone—among the many minerals that grow alongside it, heulandite-(Ca) (page 147) and apophyllite-(KF) (page 73) are the most likely to hinder identification. While the hardness, streak and colors of heulandite-(Ca) are identical to stilbite-(Ca)'s, stilbite-(Ca)'s crystals are flat, elongated and fan-shaped, and thinner at their base. In contrast, heulandite-(Ca)'s crystals are blockier. In addition, stilbite-(Ca)'s crystals aren't often found singularly, instead growing in parallel groupings referred to as "wheat-sheaf" aggregates, named for their resemblance to a bundle of wheat. Finally, apophyllite-(KF) is slightly harder, glassier and forms cubic crystals.

WHERE TO LOOK: In Washington, some of the finest crystals come from basalt in the area around Skookumchuk Dam, near Bucoda. In Oregon, vesicles in basalt at Goble are lucrative.

Soapstone

Talc (shiny green) in schist

Layered soapstone

Bright luster

Talc (tan)

Talc/Soapstone

HARDNESS: 1 **STREAK:** White

Occurrence

ENVIRONMENT: Road cuts, quarries, rivers

WHAT TO LOOK FOR: Extremely soft light-colored masses with a distinctly soapy feel

SIZE: Masses of talc and soapstone can be any size, though they are typically collected in sizes smaller than your fist

COLOR: White to gray, light to dark green, yellow to brown

OCCURRENCE: Uncommon

NOTES: Talc is virtually the softest known mineral. You can gouge it deeply with your fingernails and it can be scratched by any other mineral. This makes it one of the most easily identified minerals in all of Washington and Oregon. Aside from its extreme softness, its often greenish coloration and distinctly "soapy" or "slippery" feel are highly distinctive. Talc forms when magnesium-rich rocks and minerals, particularly serpentine (page 225) and olivine (page 189), undergo metamorphosis and are affected by hot volcanic water. Because of its metamorphic origins, talc is very rarely found crystallized and is instead more common as thick masses that are often associated with serpentine minerals. But because talc forms when large bodies of material are altered, it typically isn't found in a perfectly pure state. It is often inter-grown with chlorite minerals (page 97) and amphiboles (page 67) in large, often layered and flaky masses of rock called soapstone. Soapstone (also known as steatite) shares many traits with talc, including a very low hardness and a "soapy" feel, from which it gets its name, but it has a more uneven coloration, often with slightly harder streaks of dark green.

WHERE TO LOOK: The area around Lake Wenatchee in Washington produces talc. Dozens of areas along rivers in Josephine County, Oregon, produce both talc and soapstone.

Thomsonite-(Ca) lining basalt vesicle

Radial crystal clusters

Blade-like crystals

Thomsonite-(Ca) ball

Thomsonite-(Ca) vesicle lining

Thomsonite-(Ca)

HARDNESS: 5–5.5 **STREAK:** White

Occurrence

ENVIRONMENT: Rivers, quarries, road cuts

WHAT TO LOOK FOR: Delicate white needle-like crystals arranged into radial aggregates within vesicles (gas bubbles) in basalt

SIZE: Individual crystals are usually no more than ¼ inch long and are very thin, though groupings can measure several inches

COLOR: Colorless to white; occasionally cream to pink or brown

OCCURRENCE: Uncommon

NOTES: The Pacific Northwest is known worldwide for its abundance of zeolites, the large family of chemically complex minerals that form within cavities (especially vesicles, or gas bubbles) in basalt as it is affected by water. One of the most popular zeolites is the calcium-rich variety of thomsonite, thomsonite-(Ca). Its delicate glassy crystals make an attractive prize for diligent collectors. The crystals are typically small and needle-like and arranged into radial aggregates that are sometimes so complete and compact they are spherical or look like little "fuzz balls." A vesicle is often so filled with radial thomsonite-(Ca) groupings that they form a thick lining, sometimes even filling the cavity completely. Unfortunately, natrolite (page 185) and mesolite (page 175) form in very similar ways and generally look identical to common needle-like thomsonite-(Ca) crystals, making identification difficult. Coarse natrolite and mesolite crystals have a square cross section while large thomsonite-(Ca) crystals are flatter and blade-like in structure. However, this is not easily observed in most specimens; a lab test is sometimes the only way to definitively identify thomsonite-(Ca).

WHERE TO LOOK: The basalt formations in the areas around Spray and Goble, Oregon, are famous for zeolites. In Washington, basalt around the town of Porter is a well known source.

Luinaite-(OH) crystal cluster on quartz

Luinaite-(OH) crystal cluster on quartz

Tourmaline group

HARDNESS: 7–7.5 **STREAK:** White

Occurrence

ENVIRONMENT: Mountains, quarries

WHAT TO LOOK FOR: Very hard, dark, elongated and slender crystals with striated (grooved) sides, often embedded within rock or within minerals like feldspars and quartz

SIZE: Tourmaline-group crystals are typically smaller than an inch

COLOR: Black is common, also brown to dark green

OCCURRENCE: Uncommon in Washington; rare in Oregon

NOTES: The tourmaline group, wildly popular thanks to colorful specimens from Brazil, is a family of chemically complex minerals often resulting from metamorphic activity. Like garnets (page 133), tourmalines often develop within schist as rock is changed by heat and pressure or within very coarse volcanic rocks, such as granite (page 143). Though the tourmaline group is quite large, only three members are found in Washington and Oregon: schorl, dravite and luinaite-(OH). Schorl is technically the most common of the three, but its black, slender, striated (grooved) crystals are often very small and embedded in rock, making them easily overlooked and difficult to identify; brown dravite is less common and similarly difficult to find. Ironically, it is the rarest of the Pacific Northwest's tourmalines, luinaite-(OH), that turns up the most often in shops and collections. A relatively new mineral find that some research suggests may actually be a variety of schorl, luinaite-(OH) forms as green fiber-like crystals, often arranged into radial "sprays" on or in quartz (page 209). Often confused with amphiboles (page 67), such as hornblende, all tourmalines are harder.

WHERE TO LOOK: Mountainous regions of King and Okanogan Counties in Washington produce schorl and luinaite-(OH). In Oregon, tourmaline has rarely been found in Grant County.

243

Rough masses of tuff

Even coloration

Tuff (tan) with jasper (purple)

Obsidian fragments

Jasper

Tuff

Tuff

Occurrence

HARDNESS: N/A **STREAK:** N/A

ENVIRONMENT: Fields, road cuts, quarries

WHAT TO LOOK FOR: Soft, light-colored, gritty, porous rock containing fragments of volcanic glass and other rocks

SIZE: Tuff occurs in enormous formations

COLOR: Gray to brown, yellow

OCCURRENCE: Common

NOTES: Most igneous rocks form when molten rock cools and hardens. But any rocks that form directly due to volcanic activity are considered igneous rocks. This includes tuff, a variety of rock formed by the consolidation of ash and pulverized rock that is ejected by an explosive volcanic eruption. Given the violent volcanic history behind both Washington and Oregon, tuff is quite common in the Pacific Northwest. In some cases, tuff was produced when eruptions deposited huge amounts of ash that, over time, compacted into a soft, gritty rock. More often, however, the ash and volcanic glass associated with explosive eruptions was still very hot when it settled. The heat essentially melted the particles of ash, glass and rock together, forming welded tuff, a much harder and better-consolidated form of tuff. Both varieties are porous and can undergo induration, a process in which silica (quartz material) fills the pores and hardens the rock. Tuff is not always easy to identify, but looking for embedded pieces of volcanic glass, or obsidian (page 187), is a good clue, as is the fact that tuff is deposited as enormous formations, often visible as cliffs, hills or ridges in desert areas.

WHERE TO LOOK: One of the most spectacular formations of tuff in Oregon is Fort Rock State Park. Collecting is illegal, but the towering circular ridge of tuff is not a sight to miss. Tuff can be collected around Pleasant Valley, Oregon.

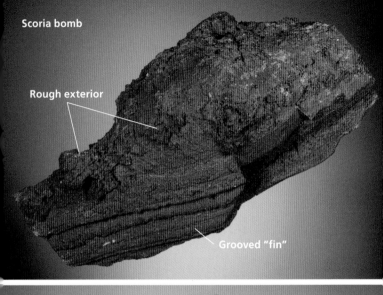

Scoria bomb

Rough exterior

Grooved "fin"

Rounded, aerodynamic shape

Volcanic bombs

HARDNESS: 5–6 **STREAK:** N/A

Occurrence

ENVIRONMENT: Fields, mountains

WHAT TO LOOK FOR: Round egg- or ball-shaped stones, often with fin-like protrusions and a very rough surface texture

SIZE: Volcanic bombs can range in size from an inch or two across to boulders several feet wide

COLOR: Brown to reddish brown, gray

OCCURRENCE: Uncommon

NOTES: Volcanic eruptions are often seen as destructive events—the disintegration of Mount St. Helens' peak during the famous 1980 eruption is a prime example of that. But eruptions actually produce more material than they destroy. Much of this material forms a volcano's pyroclastic flow, an avalanche of pulverized rock and ash that literally flows down a volcano during an eruption. Volcanic bombs, also called lava bombs, are formed when blobs of molten rock are thrown into the sky during an eruption. As the soft rock soars through the air, often as part of a pyroclastic flow, it develops a round aerodynamic shape, often complete with "fins," as it falls back to earth. Most bombs are composed of scoria, a type of gas-rich basalt (page 83) that is often reddish in color. Most are small, less than a foot in size, but some are up to ten or more feet across. They are easiest to find in desert regions where they stand out among the surrounding terrain. But if there are many rounded, weathered rocks where you're collecting, look for smooth ridges or dimples on otherwise rough, ragged surfaces of rock.

WHERE TO LOOK: Volcanic bombs turn up more frequently in Oregon, particularly central Oregon, especially near Prineville and Madras. In Washington, the areas around Mount St. Helens and Mount Rainier have specimens from more recent eruptions.

Weathered granodiorite

Diorite

Weathered diorite

Vial of volcanic ash

Coarse grains

Dacite

Volcanic rocks

HARDNESS: N/A **STREAK:** N/A

Occurrence

ENVIRONMENT: All environments

WHAT TO LOOK FOR: Dense rocks with mottled coloration, often with a large, visible grain-size

SIZE: Volcanic rocks can be found in virtually any size

COLOR: Multicolored; varies greatly, but primarily white, gray to black, tan, or brown to gray-green

OCCURRENCE: Common

NOTES: The volcanoes of the Cascade Mountain Range are still active. In fact, over the millennia they have produced countless tons of volcanic rocks. Basalt (page 83), andesite (page 71), rhyolite (page 219), and granite (page 143) are among the most abundant types of volcanic rocks, but certainly not the only ones. Diorite is a coarse-grained rock that formed within the earth, where it cooled slowly. It consists primarily of feldspars (page 123) and includes large amounts of pyroxenes (page 205) and some amphiboles (page 67), but has very little quartz (page 209) content, giving it a dark gray mottled appearance overall. Granodiorite has a similar name, but a different composition. It is a granitoid (granite-like) rock that contains more quartz than diorite and fewer dark pyroxene and amphibole minerals, resulting in a similarly coarse-grained texture but a lighter color. Dacite is one of the primary rocks produced by the infamous Mount St. Helens eruption of 1980; it is finer grained, rich in quartz and similar to rhyolite. Definitively identifying specific rocks can be difficult and often requires research and magnification.

WHERE TO LOOK: The areas around Mount St. Helens and Mount Rainier in Washington are known for volcanic rocks, but they can be found all along the Cascade Range and nearby rivers.

Aegirine (green)

Feldspar

Zircon crystal cluster
(approximately ⁵⁄₆₄" wide)

Zircon crystal
(approximately
¹⁄₅₀" long)

Albite feldspar (white)

Arfvedsonite (black)

Zircon

HARDNESS: 7.5 **STREAK:** Colorless

Occurrence

ENVIRONMENT: Mountains, road cuts

WHAT TO LOOK FOR: Tiny elongated crystals with a four-sided pyramid at each end, or small, very hard masses within rocks

SIZE: Zircon specimens are rarely larger than ⅛ inch in length

COLOR: Red to pink, off-white to yellow, brown to dark brown

OCCURRENCE: Rare in Washington; very rare in Oregon

NOTES: Zircon is an abundant mineral, but there's a catch: most zircon takes the form of nearly microscopic grains embedded in rocks, particularly granite (page 143). Zircon rarely grows to a size where it can be easily collected, but when it does, the resulting specimen is often beautiful, albeit small. Zircon's hardness is distinctive, but since most specimens from the Pacific Northwest are just a fraction of an inch in size, a scratch test is impossible to perform. Instead, you'll have to rely on observing zircon's crystal shape with the aid of magnification. When well formed, zircon crystals are elongated with a square cross section and a four-sided pyramid tipping each end, though crystals often grow upright and therefore only exhibit one pyramid tip. Color is not a distinctive feature, so if a specimen is not well crystallized and is too small to scratch, identification may nearly be impossible without a lab. The minerals found associated with a possible zircon may help, though. Crystals of feldspars (page 123), amphiboles (page 67), and pyroxenes (page 205) may all be present, especially within granite.

WHERE TO LOOK: Washington Pass in Okanogan County, Washington, is the best locality for tiny yet perfectly formed crystals within cavities in granite and granite-like rocks. In Oregon, Summit Rock in Klamath County produces tiny pink specimens often alongside pyroxenes on andesite.

Washington

Liberty Bell (right peak) and Early Winter Spires (left peak) are part of the Golden Horn Batholith, just one of the many rock formations in Washington's iconic Cascade Range.

Lush rainforests, warm ocean beaches, dry plains and snow-capped mountains are all at home in Washington, though none of these environments would exist if not for the State's dramatic geological history. As the volcanoes erupted and coastlines shifted to create the varied terrain we see in Washington today, stunning crystals were forming, rocks were weathering, and ancient animals were being fossilized. These spectacular acts of nature have developed Washington's reputation as a rock hounding destination.

Skilled collectors flock to the Cascade Mountain Range where some of the world's rarest minerals hide within solid granite, while casual hobbyists stroll the beaches of Puget Sound looking for interesting stones to take home as a souvenir. Every corner of Washington yields some kind of geological treasure for rock and mineral collectors, and some people have even been fortunate enough to discover world-class specimens in Washington. With some research, diligence, and an adventurous spirit, the Evergreen State will reward you as well.

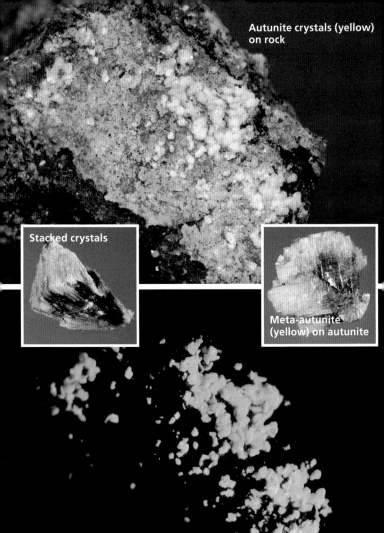

Autunite crystals (yellow) on rock

Stacked crystals

Meta-autunite (yellow) on autunite

Same specimen as above under short-wave ultraviolet light

Autunite/Meta-autunite

HARDNESS: 2–2.5 **STREAK:** Pale yellow

Occurrence

ENVIRONMENT: Quarries

WHAT TO LOOK FOR: Radioactive, bright yellow-green, flat and square plate-like crystals that fluoresce in ultraviolet light

SIZE: Most autunite crystals are smaller than ½ inch

COLOR: Autunite yellow-green to green; meta-autunite yellow

OCCURRENCE: Very rare

NOTES: Autunite is easily one of the most attractive and most famous of Washington's minerals, but you won't likely be able to collect it yourself. The mines that once produced world-class specimens of this mineral have long been closed, but Washington specimens of autunite are easy to buy, so Washington rock hounds should still be familiar with it. Autunite is a uranium ore and is radioactive, but typically only mildly so. It is often found as perfectly formed crystals that appear as thin, flat, plate-like squares. Frequently, so many of these square crystals have grown side-by-side that they form layered blocks that sometimes slightly fan out like the pages of a partially opened book. The yellow-green crystals are also fluorescent under ultraviolet light, making identification simple. Meta-autunite, which was first discovered in Washington, is the partially dehydrated form of autunite and is a distinct mineral. It typically forms on top of autunite as a yellow crust, often visible as a yellow "rind" on the edges of greener autunite crystals.

WHERE TO LOOK: Many places in eastern Washington produced specimens, but the Daybreak Mine on Mount Kit Carson in Spokane County is considered one of the world's best sources for museum-quality autunite, but the mines are closed today. It is possible that the surrounding area could once again produce autunite specimens.

Quartz

Boulangerite (metallic gray)

Boulangerite masses

Crystals in quartz

Close-up of intergrown needle-like crystals

Boulangerite

HARDNESS: 2.5–3 **STREAK:** Brownish gray

Occurrence

ENVIRONMENT: Quarries, mountains

WHAT TO LOOK FOR: Very soft, dark, metallic mineral that easily blackens your hands, often embedded in rock or quartz and exhibits a fibrous appearance

SIZE: Masses of boulangerite can be several inches in size, though individual crystals tend to be shorter than ¼ inch

COLOR: Dark gray to black, bluish gray

OCCURRENCE: Very rare

NOTES: Boulangerite is a rare Washington collectible, and is somewhat famous from the eastern portion of the state thanks to some well-formed specimens from a few old mines. But few localities still yield boulangerite, so unless you do your homework you're not likely to find it. Boulangerite does frequently turn up in shops and collections, so it's still worth being familiar with. An ore of lead, boulangerite is a soft, metallic mineral that, when very well crystallized, appears as fibers or needles. The vast majority of specimens are embedded masses, however, and often exhibit a fibrous or splintery appearance, indicative of the crystals that comprise a mass. In addition, many specimens will blacken your hands after handling. This can be distinctive, but be sure to wash your hands well as boulangerite contains lead and antimony. It frequently occurs with galena (page 263), with which it can be easily confused; both are very soft, but boulangerite's brown streak will help. Stibnite (page 235) is also similar, but is softer and more widespread.

WHERE TO LOOK: Only a handful of old mines produce boulangerite, primarily those in Stevens County and other locations in eastern Washington, where it is often embedded in quartzite or sedimentary rocks.

Well-formed crystal group

Stubby crystal

Blocky clinozoisite crystals (tan to brown) on skarn with diopside (green)

Clinozoisite

HARDNESS: 7 **STREAK:** Light gray

ENVIRONMENT: Mountains, quarries

Occurrence

WHAT TO LOOK FOR: Elongated, glassy, translucent yellow-brown crystals with striated (grooved) faces in metamorphic rock

SIZE: Clinozoisite crystals are rarely longer than an inch

COLOR: Brown to yellow-brown, honey yellow, greenish to gray

OCCURRENCE: Rare

NOTES: Clinozoisite is a rare member of the epidote group (page 119) that is found in very few places in Washington. Nevertheless, it is still worth mentioning because of the very fine quality of crystals sometimes found in the state. It forms primarily in metamorphic rocks, particularly skarn (page 233), a coarse-grained rock that forms when limestone contacts molten granite. Clinozoisite develops fine crystals within cavities in its host rock; its crystals are elongated and rectangular, typically thin and striated (grooved) along their length. They are often terminated, or tipped, with a short angular point, though this trait is not always present depending on how much space a crystal had when it formed. This shape and occurrence in metamorphic rocks is distinctive, as is its high hardness, translucence, and yellow-brown coloration. You could confuse clinozoisite with poorly formed garnet (page 133), with which it often forms, but garnet is more common and generally rounder. Epidote can also look very similar but is more common, more deeply striated, and typically greener. Finally, because of their similar hardness, clinozoisite can be confused with the tourmalines (page 243), but tourmalines are rarely translucent.

WHERE TO LOOK: The area around Vesper Peak in Snohomish County produces the best crystals in the state, which are embedded within metamorphic rocks alongside garnets.

Fluorite fragments

Backlit specimen

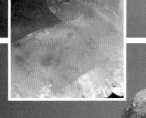

Impurity-rich outer crystal surface

Crystal growth ridges

Fluorite

HARDNESS: 4 **STREAK:** White

ENVIRONMENT: Quarries

Occurrence

WHAT TO LOOK FOR: Soft, glassy, light-colored masses that often exhibit triangular or square features and can be easily scratched by a knife but not by a U.S. nickel

SIZE: Fluorite crystals are rarely larger than a thumbnail while masses can rarely measure up to a few inches

COLOR: Colorless to white, green to yellow, rarely pink to purple

OCCURRENCE: Very rare

NOTES: Fluorite, the primary source of the element fluorine, is normally a fairly common mineral in most states, but in much of the Pacific Northwest, the geology just isn't right. Parts of Washington, however, have produced the mineral, but access to collector-quality specimens is very limited. When well formed, fluorite crystals take the form of cubes, octahedrons (an eight-faced shape resembling two pyramids placed base-to-base), or a combination of the two, often hiding within cavities in granite. Most specimens from Washington are poorly crystallized, if crystallized at all. Instead, they form as glassy, pale green masses and exhibit blocky, square-like growth ridges or triangular internal fracturing, both features derived from fluorite's crystal structure. Identifying fluorite is easy as its hardness is very distinctive. This distinguishes it from calcite (page 85), which is softer, and from colored varieties of quartz (page 209), which are harder. Finding it requires research and effort.

WHERE TO LOOK: Masses of fluorite were produced at several mines in Stevens County, though most sites are off-limits and specimens from the area are primarily procured via mineral dealers. Granite at Washington Pass in Okanogan County rarely produces beautiful tiny crystals.

261

Masses of galena

Bright luster

Close-up of galena mass

Galena

HARDNESS: 2.5 **STREAK:** Lead gray

ENVIRONMENT: Mountains, quarries

Occurrence

WHAT TO LOOK FOR: Dark-colored, soft, and very heavy metallic mineral exhibiting high luster, often with a blocky structure

SIZE: Most galena specimens are palm-sized and smaller

COLOR: Dark lead-gray

OCCURRENCE: Uncommon

NOTES: Lead, the extremely dense and notoriously toxic metallic element, is primarily obtained by mining galena, a mixture of lead and sulfur. Luckily for rock hounds, galena's sulfur content makes it relatively safe to handle, though you'll still want to be careful around dust produced from it. Galena is widespread throughout central and eastern Washington, but only in small amounts. Frequently found embedded in granite or sedimentary rocks like limestone, galena forms as perfect cubes when well crystallized, but massive or compact granular specimens are far more common. It is always a dark lead-gray color and is always metallic, though some specimens are far more lustrous than others. While stibnite (page 235), boulangerite (page 257), and arsenopyrite (page 77) may look similar, galena's hardness and streak color are quite distinctive. To further identify it, take note of a specimen's weight. Galena's lead content makes the mineral so dense that even small specimens feel very heavy for their size. In addition, galena has cubic cleavage, which means that a specimen will break into perfect cubes when struck, a trait often visible in specimens with blocky, step-like shapes.

WHERE TO LOOK: The vast majority of Washington's galena specimens come from Chelan, Ferry and Okanogan Counties and occur as embedded masses in quartz or various rock types, primarily granite, serpentinite and sedimentary rocks.

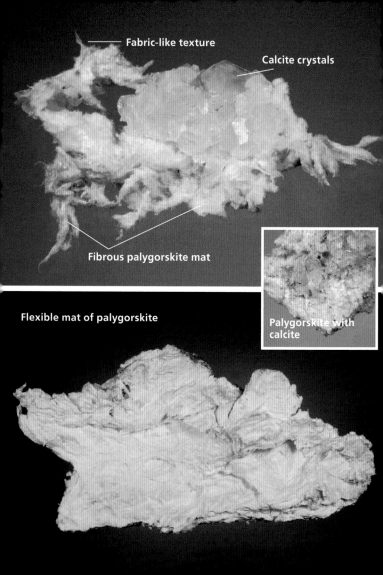

Fabric-like texture

Calcite crystals

Fibrous palygorskite mat

Palygorskite with calcite

Flexible mat of palygorskite

Palygorskite

HARDNESS: 2–2.5 **STREAK:** White

Occurrence

ENVIRONMENT: Mountains, quarries

WHAT TO LOOK FOR: Very soft, flexible, fabric-like sheets of material, often intergrown with crystals of calcite (page 85)

SIZE: Palygorskite occurs in sheets that can measure several inches across, though most specimens are palm-sized

COLOR: White to gray common, occasionally yellow to brown

OCCURRENCE: Very rare

NOTES: Palygorskite, also known as attapulgite, is one of Washington's most compelling minerals, but is also one that the average rock hound will probably never be able to collect themselves. It is technically a clay mineral (page 103), but unlike the clay you may be familiar with, palygorskite forms as intergrown mats of fiber-like crystals that are so soft and flexible that they look and feel like fabric. Nicknamed "mountain leather," these fibrous formations of palygorskite are a type of asbestos, though they are not typically considered dangerous; however, when working with this material, it's still a good idea to wear a respirator. Washington's palygorskite formed in the Metaline Falls area within cavities in limestone (page 165), and specimens are often intergrown with transparent calcite crystals (page 85). Specimens were produced from zinc and lead mines, and though most known locations are inaccessible today, it may still be possible to find palygorskite in the area. Thanks to its unique appearance, you won't confuse it with anything else.

WHERE TO LOOK: Metaline Falls in Pend Oreille County is the only area that produced specimen-quality palygorskite, but most samples came from within now-closed zinc and lead mines. It might still be possible to find specimens in cavities in limestone in the surrounding area.

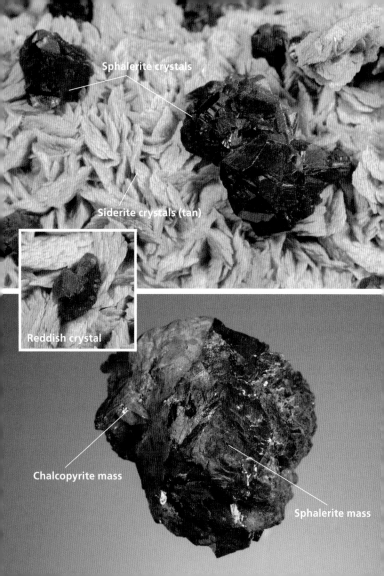

Sphalerite crystals

Siderite crystals (tan)

Reddish crystal

Chalcopyrite mass

Sphalerite mass

Sphalerite

HARDNESS: 3.5–4 **STREAK:** Light brown

Occurrence

ENVIRONMENT: Mountains, quarries, road cuts

WHAT TO LOOK FOR: Brightly lustrous, often dark-colored crystals with many triangular faces, or masses occurring with chalcopyrite or siderite

SIZE: Sphalerite crystals are typically smaller than a thumbnail, while masses can be up to a few inches in size

COLOR: Reddish brown to black, yellow to greenish yellow

OCCURRENCE: Uncommon

NOTES: Sphalerite is the world's primary source of zinc, and is a mineral that all rock hounds should be familiar with. Frequently occurring alongside chalcopyrite (page 93) and other sulfur-bearing minerals, sphalerite typically forms when volcanic water deposits minerals in cavities and veins in rock, but it can also form via a sedimentary process in limestone, though this is less common in the Pacific Northwest. It is often found crystallized, though rarely in fine crystals. Well-formed crystals often take the shape of a three-sided pyramid or a twelve-faced ball-like formation, but sphalerite's crystal faces are often curved or "bulging," complicating identification. In addition, crystals are often twinned, or intergrown within each other, making a specimen appear as if it has too many or too few faces. With such crystals or massive, non-crystallized specimens, you'll have to rely on other means of identification. Sphalerite's hardness is distinctive when found in conjunction with a specimen with a high luster, a brownish red to yellow coloration, triangular crystal faces, and a light brown streak.

WHERE TO LOOK: The Snoqualmie River area in King County, Washington, produces attractive crystals on siderite. Sphalerite is also found in dozens of locations in Ferry County.

Stilpnomelane formations (black) in quartz (white)

Stilpnomelane in green jasper

Perfectly formed crystal cluster

Shiny black stilpnomelane formations in quartz

Stilpnomelane

HARDNESS: 3–4 **STREAK:** Pale gray

Occurrence

ENVIRONMENT: Mountains, road cuts

WHAT TO LOOK FOR: Round, flaky, black and highly lustrous mineral formations embedded in quartz or jasper

SIZE: Individual stilpnomelane formations are typically pea-sized while masses can measure several inches

COLOR: Black to dark brown, rarely dark green

OCCURRENCE: Rare

NOTES: Stilpnomelane, named from the Greek words *stilpnos* (shining) and *melanos* (black), is a rare Washington mineral only found in a few locations. Much like a mica (page 177), it forms as thin, flat, sheet-like crystals, but unlike the micas, stilpnomelane's crystals are typically arranged into almost spherical groupings in which individual crystals radiate outward from a central point. These round formations are often intergrown to form large masses or veins, and the individual leaf-like crystals within them give specimens a flaky appearance. As its name implies, stilpnomelane is almost always black (though some samples can be dark brown or greenish). It is brightly lustrous, sometimes even appearing metallic, even though it's not actually a metallic mineral. It forms within schist, and in Washington it is generally found embedded within quartz or green-gray jasper veins where it is very conspicuous. Due to its rarity and unique appearance, you won't likely confuse it for anything else. If you do, it will probably be a mica, but all micas are softer. Though unlikely, you could confuse it with hematite, but hematite always has a reddish-brown streak.

WHERE TO LOOK: Blanchard Mountain, approximately five miles south of Bellingham in Skagit County, yields quartz veins containing the best stilpnomelane formations in the state.

Small (⅛")
zektzerite crystal
(glassy tan)

Feldspar (dull tan)

Crude zektzerite crystals

Same specimen as above under short-wave ultraviolet light

Zektzerite

HARDNESS: 6 **STREAK:** White

ENVIRONMENT: Mountains

Occurrence

WHAT TO LOOK FOR: Tiny light-colored crystals that appear hexagonal (six-sided) in shape and are found on feldspar in pockets within granite

SIZE: Zektzerite crystals are always smaller than ¼ inch, with most specimens measuring less than ¹⁄₁₆ inch

COLOR: Colorless to white, cream to yellow, rarely pink

OCCURRENCE: Very rare

NOTES: Zektzerite is one of Washington's type minerals, which means that it was first discovered in the state. In fact, the type locality, Washington Pass in Okanogan County, is one of only four locations in the world where zektzerite is found. This extremely rare lithium-bearing mineral forms within small cavities in the granite found at the pass. Its crystals are pseudohexagonal, which means that they appear to be hexagonal (six-sided), even though they don't actually have a hexagonal internal structure. Though perfect examples of these glassy crystals turn up, most zektzerite specimens consist of more poorly formed shapes, exhibiting just one or two crystal faces grown atop microcline feldspar (page 123). Crystals are often stacked or grown side-by-side, giving a specimen the appearance of faint parallel lines. Zektzerite specimens vary in color; pink crystals are highly prized, but most specimens are colorless to cream or yellow, sometimes perfectly matching the color of the feldspar they have grown upon. Finally, zektzerite is fluorescent green to blue under short-wave ultraviolet light.

WHERE TO LOOK: Washington Pass in Okanogan County is the only locality and zektzerite can be found within granite boulders. The area is a national forest, however.

Oregon

The rugged coastline at Bandon is a stunning example of Oregon's famous Pacific Coast, which provides a stunning backdrop for collecting agates, jaspers and fossils, three of the most popular rock hounding activities along Oregon's shores.

Among rock and mineral collectors, Oregon is widely known as one of the premier collecting locations in the western United States. Beds of colorful jaspers, pockets of delicate zeolites, forests of petrified wood, and entire mountains of volcanic glass beckon rock hounds to visit the Beaver State to search for precious discoveries of their own. But it isn't just what you can add to your collection that makes Oregon worth a visit. The rugged Pacific Coast, the stunning Columbia River Gorge, and the ancient Wallowa Mountains are just a few examples of the geological beauty Oregon has to offer.

Born out of the Pacific Ocean from eruptions of molten rock, today, Oregon is a place of extremes. The cool western forests give way to the soaring peaks of the Cascade Mountain Range that fade into the expansive dry deserts of the east. These great variations in terrain are not only an indicator of the diverse assortment of collectibles that are found in the state, but also a preview of the endless adventures ambitious collectors can embark upon in Oregon.

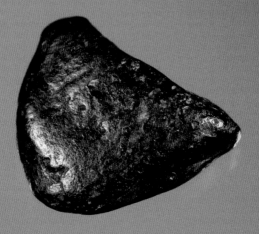

Water-worn awaruite nugget (½") with brown surface coating

Water-worn awaruite nugget (¾") with reddish surface coating

Awaruite (Josephinite)

HARDNESS: 5–5.5 **STREAK:** Gray

Occurrence

ENVIRONMENT: Rivers

WHAT TO LOOK FOR: Silvery metallic nuggets or grains, often with a brown surface coating, which are highly magnetic and are found at the bottom of Josephine Creek in Oregon

SIZE: Awaruite occurs in nuggets and grains rarely larger than your thumbnail and typically much smaller

COLOR: Silvery white to gray; often with a brown surface coating

OCCURRENCE: Very rare

NOTES: Awaruite is not only one of Oregon's rarest minerals, but it is also one of the most interesting. It gets its name from the locality in Australia where it was first discovered, but it is also called josephinite (particularly in older texts) for Josephine Creek in southwestern Oregon where some of the world's most significant examples of this rare mineral have been found. In fact, this is the only river in Oregon in which awaruite nuggets and rounded grains can be found. But what makes awaruite so unique is its chemical composition; it consists of an alloy of nickel and iron. This rare mixture of metals only combines to form awaruite within certain rocks, such as the heavily metamorphosed serpentine-rich rocks the Josephine River flows across. Though a rather obscure and rare mineral, awaruite isn't very difficult to identify. It is typically a silvery metallic gray, but it often has a brown surface coating caused by the weathering of its iron content. It's also very malleable (bendable) and harder than similar metals, like silver. But perhaps its most diagnostic trait is its strong magnetism; other magnetic minerals will not share the rest of its traits.

WHERE TO LOOK: The only locality is Josephine Creek in Josephine County in southwestern Oregon, near the California border.

Cavansite crystal clusters (blue)

Cavansite vein

Analcime

Cavansite (blue)

Radial "sprays"

Cavansite

HARDNESS: 3–4 **STREAK:** Light blue to white

Occurrence

ENVIRONMENT: Road cuts

WHAT TO LOOK FOR: Tiny, thin and elongated bright blue crystals, often arranged into radial "sprays" within cavities in basalt

SIZE: Individual crystals are tiny, typically no more than an eighth of an inch in length; groupings can grow slightly larger

COLOR: Light to dark blue, bluish green

OCCURRENCE: Very rare

NOTES: Cavansite is a very unique Oregon mineral. Not only is it one of the state's most beautiful and colorful minerals, cavansite is also one of Oregon's type minerals, which means that it was first discovered in the state. It is also one of the rarest minerals in Oregon, and the majority of collectors will never find a specimen. In fact, most extant specimens were found decades ago, though that doesn't mean there aren't more samples to find. Unlike stilbite-(Ca) (page 237) or chabazite-(Ca) (page 89), cavansite is not a zeolite, but it forms alongside zeolites in the same vesicles (gas bubbles) and cavities that they do. Cavansite forms as tiny elongated crystals, but they rarely form alone. Instead, they arrange themselves into radial "spray"-shaped aggregates, sometimes so well formed in all directions that they resemble small spheres. Though several zeolites form this way as well, cavansite's characteristic bright blue color distinguishes it from all minerals that may share a similar appearance. Other blue minerals in Oregon will differ in hardness or will not be found in vesicles.

WHERE TO LOOK: Virtually the only known locality is the north end of Owyhee Lake, near Owyhee Dam in Malheur County, Oregon. Beware: parts of this area are now a state park and you'll have to determine where you can and can't collect.

Green garnierite mass

Brecciated garnierite

Close-up of texture

Limonite (orange)

Garnierite on botryoidal chalcedony

Garnierite

HARDNESS: N/A **STREAK:** White to pale green

ENVIRONMENT: Quarries, rivers

Occurrence

WHAT TO LOOK FOR: Vivid green masses, sometimes with a botryoidal (grape-like) surface and often intergrown with quartz (page 209), limonite (page 167), or serpentine (page 225)

SIZE: Garnierite occurs massively and can be found in many sizes, though specimens are normally smaller than a fist

COLOR: Light to dark green, bluish green

OCCURRENCE: Rare

NOTES: Much in the same way that the name "limonite" is used to describe mixtures of iron-bearing minerals, "garnierite" is used to denote massive mixtures of nickel-bearing minerals. Because of the high nickel content of the minerals that comprise garnierite—primarily népouite, pimelite and willemseite—it is found in vivid shades of green, making it highly sought after. It is often found as soft, chalky masses embedded within rock or limonite, but its hardness is not distinctive as it is often intergrown with other minerals, particularly quartz (page 209) and chalcedony (page 91). This can make it appear harder than it actually is. It can also appear as botryoidal (grape-like) growths, though this is also often a result of it forming atop another mineral. Garnierite can be easily confused with chrysocolla (page 99) and celadonite (page 87), but chrysocolla is virtually always more blue in color and celadonite forms in vesicles (gas bubbles) in basalt, while garnierite does not. Garnierite forms when peridotite, a rare olivine-rich rock, is weathered in wet, tropical conditions, giving insight into Oregon's past.

WHERE TO LOOK: The area around Riddle, Oregon, in Douglas County produces the most specimens, particularly from the dumps at old mines, but be mindful of private property.

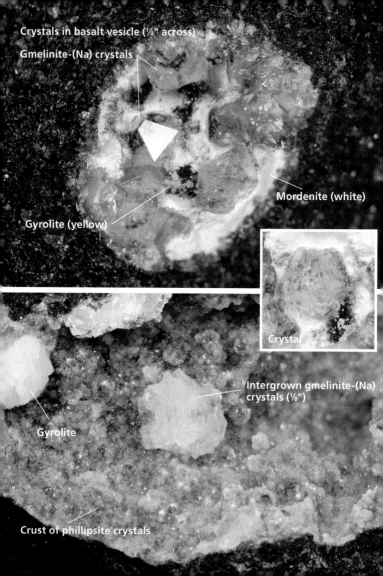

Crystals in basalt vesicle (⅛" across)

Gmelinite-(Na) crystals

Gyrolite (yellow)

Mordenite (white)

Crystal

Intergrown gmelinite-(Na) crystals (⅛")

Gyrolite

Crust of phillipsite crystals

Gmelinite-(Na)

HARDNESS: 4.5 **STREAK:** White

Occurrence

ENVIRONMENT: Road cuts, quarries, rivers

WHAT TO LOOK FOR: Tiny hexagonal (six-sided) clear, glassy crystals that sometimes seem to be "missing" their tip, grown within vesicles (gas bubbles) in basalt, often with gyrolite

SIZE: Gmelinite-(Na) crystals are typically smaller than ⅛ inch

COLOR: Colorless to white or gray

OCCURRENCE: Very rare

NOTES: Gmelinite-(Na), the sodium-rich member of the gmelinite mineral series, is one of Oregon's rarest zeolites. The zeolite group is a family of complex minerals that typically form within vesicles (gas bubbles) in basalt or other igneous rocks affected by alkaline, mineral-rich groundwater. Unlike many of the region's zeolites, which form as tiny needle-like crystals, gmelinite-(Na)'s crystals are stout and hexagonal (six-sided) with rectangular faces. The tops of the crystals often taper and end with a flat tip, but many specimens instead exhibit an inverse point, appearing as a funnel-shaped cavity at the crystal's top. This "missing" tip often leads inexperienced collectors to believe a specimen is broken. These crystal traits are very distinctive, especially in conjunction with its coloration, which is typically colorless with internal white or gray coloration. Gmelinite-(Na) can be confused with other zeolites, particularly analcime (page 69) or poorly formed phillipsite (page 197), or other hexagonal minerals like quartz (page 209). But analcime is harder, phillipsite is slightly softer, more flat and rectangular in shape, and quartz is much harder and more common.

WHERE TO LOOK: The only known locality is basalt in the Devil's Backbone area along the North Fork of the John Day River, southwest of Ukiah in Grant County.

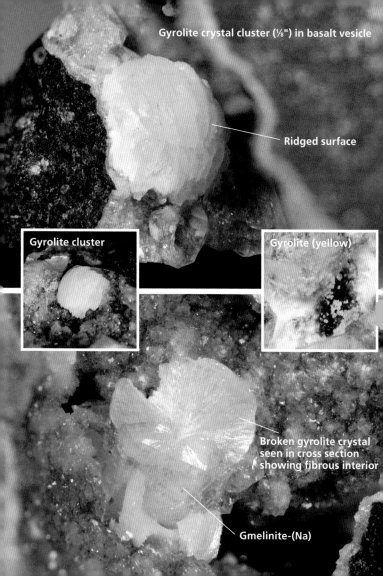

Gyrolite crystal cluster (⅛") in basalt vesicle

Ridged surface

Gyrolite cluster

Gyrolite (yellow)

Broken gyrolite crystal seen in cross section showing fibrous interior

Gmelinite-(Na)

Gyrolite

HARDNESS: 2.5 **STREAK:** White

ENVIRONMENT: Quarries, road cuts, rivers

Occurrence

WHAT TO LOOK FOR: Small, white ball-like formations within vesicles (gas bubbles) or veins in basalt

SIZE: Gyrolite specimens are rarely larger than ¼ inch

COLOR: Colorless to white, sometimes yellow to brown

OCCURRENCE: Rare

NOTES: Gyrolite is one of the many minerals that form within vesicles (gas bubbles) in basalt in Oregon. Though gyrolite is not a member of the zeolite group (the large family of minerals that form within vesicles when basalt is altered by alkaline groundwater), it is closely related to them and occurs in the same environments. It can even be found within the same vesicle as zeolites like analcime (page 69) and natrolite (page 185). Gyrolite forms as spherical crystal clusters and individual crystals are never seen. These clusters are typically white and appear smooth to the naked eye, but under magnification you can often observe a surface composed of short ridges. When broken in half, the cross section of a gyrolite growth has a fibrous radial structure. These traits are fairly distinctive, but formations of mordenite (page 181), thomsonite-(Ca) (page 241), and other zeolites can look nearly identical. However, because they consist of needle-like individual crystals, round clusters of zeolites often have a "fuzzy" appearance, especially under magnification. Gyrolite formations are composed of plate-like crystals, not needle-like crystals, hence the ridges seen on gyrolite spheres under magnification. Finally, most zeolites are more common than gyrolite.

WHERE TO LOOK: Zeolite-bearing basalt near Ritter in Grant County and near Spray in Wheeler County produce gyrolite.

Mansfieldite in tuff

Mansfieldite
(darker gray)

Mansfieldite in tuff

Mansfieldite

Tuff matrix

Mansfieldite

HARDNESS: 3.5–4 **STREAK:** White

Occurrence

ENVIRONMENT: Mountains, quarries

WHAT TO LOOK FOR: Irregular glassy gray crusts within cavities in tuff on Hubart Butte

SIZE: Crusts of mansfieldite are tiny, often no more than ¼ inch

COLOR: White to gray, rarely pale greenish gray

OCCURRENCE: Very rare

NOTES: A few Oregon minerals are only found in one place, and mansfieldite is among them. Named for an important geologist, mansfieldite is a very rare aluminum- and arsenic-bearing mineral that is only known to occur on Hobart Butte in Lane County. Safe to collect when handled briefly, it does not form crystals in Oregon. Instead, it appears as crusts and irregular masses within cavities in tuff (page 245), often with a colloform structure (a surface comprised of small lumps). Some growths are elongated and ropey, not unlike the appearance of melted wax. Typically white to gray in color, rarely with a greenish tint, mansfieldite formations would be completely inconspicuous within tuff if not for their bright glassy luster. This lustrous appearance contrasts against the dull rock; under magnification, translucency can often be observed in mansfieldite as well, further distinguishing it. Because of its distinct appearance and its rarity, there won't be anything else you're likely to mistake it for. Quartz (page 209) is one of the only other glassy white minerals to occur at Hobart Butte, but is frequently crystallized and is much harder than mansfieldite.

WHERE TO LOOK: Hobart Butte, west of Drain in Lane County, is the only locality, but beware of private property in the area.

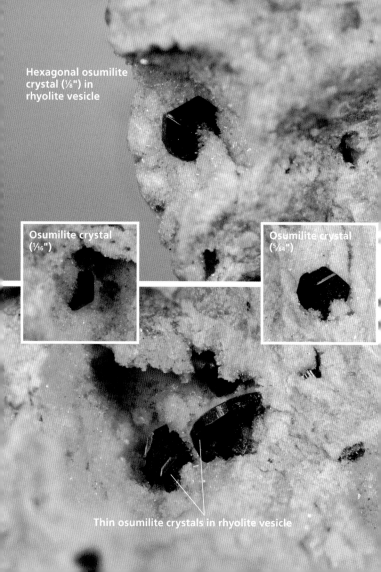

Hexagonal osumilite crystal (⅛") in rhyolite vesicle

Osumilite crystal (1/16")

Osumilite crystal (5/64")

Thin osumilite crystals in rhyolite vesicle

Osumilite

HARDNESS: 5–6 **STREAK:** Pale blue-gray

ENVIRONMENT: Mountains, quarries

WHAT TO LOOK FOR: Tiny, flat six-sided crystals, with a fairly high hardness and dark blue coloration, within rhyolite vesicles

SIZE: Most osumilite crystals are smaller than ⅛ inch in width

COLOR: Dark blue to black

OCCURRENCE: Very rare

NOTES: Osumilite is an extremely rare mineral that is found in only a few places around the world and in only one location in the United States—North Sister Mountain in Oregon. Sadly for rock hounds, this site is now protected, but specimens are still frequently available for sale, and it is always possible that another locality for this mineral will be discovered, so familiarize yourself with osumilite. Aside from its rarity, osumilite is also highly sought after due to the fact that its tiny crystals are often perfectly formed. Crystals always take the form of flat hexagonal (six-sided) plates and are found tucked inside vesicles (gas bubbles) and fissures in rhyolite. Its glassy and lustrous crystals often grow on one end, so not all of a crystal's sides are always visible. Most specimens are a very dark blue, often so dark they appear black. Osumilite is so rare that you won't confuse it for anything else (provided that you examine it under magnification), but on first glance it may resemble hexagonal crystals of micas (page 177). All mica minerals are much softer, however, and they are much thinner than osumilite crystals. Osumilite could also resemble some pyroxenes (page 205) or amphiboles (page 67), but none are blue.

WHERE TO LOOK: The only location is the Obsidian Cliffs on North Sister Mountain in Lane County, but unfortunately for collectors, the area is now a protected national forest.

White clay

Individual paulingite-(Ca) crystal
(approximately 3/64" wide)

Stack of intergrown crystals
(approximately 13/32" long)

Paulingite-(Ca)

HARDNESS: 5 **STREAK:** White

ENVIRONMENT: Road cuts

Occurrence

WHAT TO LOOK FOR: Tiny, colorless, faceted ball-like crystals with a six-sided outline within vesicles (gas bubbles) in basalt

SIZE: Crystals are tiny and never larger than an eighth of an inch

COLOR: Colorless to white

OCCURRENCE: Very rare

NOTES: With only one known locality, paulingite-(Ca) is easily one of the rarest minerals in the Pacific Northwest, and only the most ambitious, persistent, and well-researched rock hounds will find this elusive mineral. But there is good reason to track down paulingite-(Ca); its crystals are typically very well developed and they can be found in incredible formations, such as precarious stacks or chains of intergrown crystals. Paulingite-(Ca) is a zeolite mineral, of which there are well over a dozen in Oregon. Like all zeolites, it forms within vesicles (gas bubbles) in basalt as the rock is affected by alkaline groundwater. But you won't confuse paulingite-(Ca) with other zeolites if well-formed crystals are present (though you will need magnification to see them). That's because paulingite-(Ca) forms tiny rhombic dodecahedrons, which are twelve-faced crystals that resemble faceted balls, and no other zeolite in Oregon forms like this. Each of the twelve crystal faces on a crystal are diamond-shaped, which can make identification easy. When intergrown or poorly formed, you could confuse it with phillipsite (page 197), but phillipsite has more elongated, rectangular crystals. Garnets (page 133) also share this crystal shape, but all are harder.

WHERE TO LOOK: Paulingite-(Ca) is only known to exist in vesicles in basalt near Threemile Creek, west of Ritter in Grant County, Oregon.

Unpolished snakeskin "agates" with chalky surface coating

Polished specimen

Pink-gray coloration

Multiple lobes

Polished snakeskin "agates"

Snakeskin "agate"

HARDNESS: ~7 **STREAK:** White

ENVIRONMENT: Fields, road cuts

Occurrence

WHAT TO LOOK FOR: Rounded masses with lobe-like growths, a cracked chalky exterior, and a hard gray interior

SIZE: Snakeskin agates can be found as large as a grapefruit, but most are fist-sized and smaller

COLOR: Exterior white to gray or brown; interior light to dark gray, bluish gray, pale brown to pink

OCCURRENCE: Rare

NOTES: Snakeskin agates are a popular Oregon collectible, but their name is a misnomer and a collector's term. While snakeskin agates do have a web-like, channeled appearance reminiscent of snake skin, they are not actually agates (page 47) at all. Studies have shown that they are actually composed of chert (page 95), which formed by a sedimentary process when an ancient, highly alkaline lake evaporated. The chert features many rounded structures, including lobes and knob-like protrusions; the "snake skin" is a cracked chalky coating that is softer, lighter and formed on the surface of the chert. Collectors often polish specimens until most, but not all, of the outer layer is removed, accentuating the snakeskin-like appearance and exposing the hard gray or pink interior. Specimens are found only near Rome, Oregon, in a flat desert region composed primarily of mudstone (page 183) and tuff (page 245). Specimens are often loose on the surface where they are conspicuous as hard white masses. Because of their unique features and rarity, you won't likely confuse them with any other mineral formation.

WHERE TO LOOK: Snakeskin agates are found in Malheur County, approximately 6 miles southwest of Rome, Oregon. The area is a desert, however, so do not go unprepared.

Crust of intergrown stellerite crystals

Cross section

Ball-like stellerite formation

Pearly luster

Stellerite

HARDNESS: 4.5 **STREAK:** White

ENVIRONMENT: Rivers

Occurrence

WHAT TO LOOK FOR: Thick veins of pearly intergrown crystals found lining fissures at Ritter Hot Springs, in Grant County

SIZE: Masses of crystals can measure several inches across

COLOR: White to cream-colored, yellow to light brown

OCCURRENCE: Very rare

NOTES: Stellerite is a zeolite; zeolites are chemically complex water-bearing minerals that form within vesicles (gas bubbles) in basalt affected by alkaline groundwater. But stellerite is unique in Oregon. It is only found in one location in the entire state—Ritter Hot Springs—where it doesn't form in basalt vesicles. Instead, it forms within fissures in the rock of the hot spring itself. It is deposited on the walls of the spring by the warm mineral-rich water rising from the earth. When this occurrence of stellerite was first discovered in 1915, the material was originally thought to be stilbite-(Ca) (page 237), due to their similar chemical composition and luster. Despite the fact that the stellerite from Ritter Hot Springs forms in thick crusts of heavily intergrown crystals and the structure of individual crystals cannot be seen, its occurrence in the hot springs is so unique that it is no longer confused with stilbite-(Ca). In the hot springs, the stellerite occurs with calcite (page 85), which can even be sandwiched between two growths of stellerite. Unfortunately, you won't be able to collect stellerite for yourself because the area is privately owned, though nearby areas could produce specimens as well.

WHERE TO LOOK: The only known location is Ritter Hot Springs in Grant County, though this area (including the hot spring) is now private property.

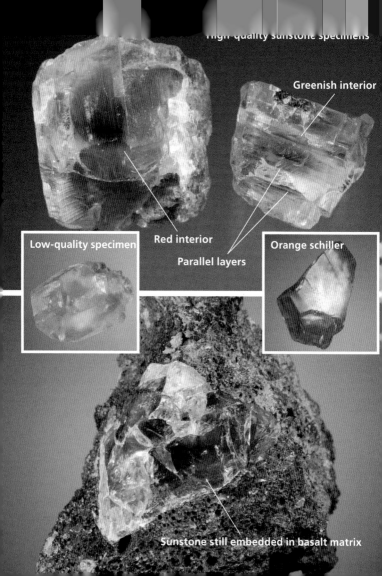

High-quality sunstone specimens

Greenish interior

Red interior

Parallel layers

Low-quality specimen

Orange schiller

Sunstone still embedded in basalt matrix

Sunstone

HARDNESS: 6–6.5 **STREAK:** White

ENVIRONMENT: Quarries

WHAT TO LOOK FOR: Hard, transparent, glassy yellow fragments, often with red centers or an orange schiller (a shimmer)

SIZE: Most sunstone specimens are no larger than an inch or two

COLOR: Colorless to yellow or pale green common; pale to dark red, green, copper-orange rare, occasionally multicolored

OCCURRENCE: Very rare

NOTES: The word "sunstone" is a collectors' term used to describe gem-grade specimens of transparent feldspars (page 123) that contain tiny internal growths of other minerals that cause a schiller, or metallic shimmer, from within. Found in various places throughout the world, sunstone's distinctive schiller is usually caused by tiny hematite crystals (page 145) deep within the feldspar, but Oregon's sunstone is unique. Widely regarded as the best sunstone in the United States, Oregon sunstone consists of transparent yellow labradorite or oligoclase feldspar that contains nearly microscopic flecks of copper, creating a distinct orange or reddish metallic sheen from within a specimen. It forms as large embedded masses in porphyritic basalt (page 199), but often weathers free and can be found lying loose on the surface as irregular glassy chunks. High-grade specimens have red or green centers, while low-quality specimens are just transparent yellow in color.

WHERE TO LOOK: Sunstones are only found in Harney County and near Plush in Lake County. Most known localities are privately owned, but several near Plush operate pay-to-dig services. A state-owned public collection site is located in a desert north of Plush—information is available from the Bureau of Land Management at www.blm.gov/or.

Relatively large (⁷⁄₆₄") steeply pointed single crystal in basalt vesicle

Clay

Tiny vesicle lined with crystals

Tiny (³⁄₆₄") glass-clear cluster of crystals in clay-lined basalt vesicle

Tschernichite

HARDNESS: 4.5 **STREAK:** White

Occurrence

ENVIRONMENT: Road cuts

WHAT TO LOOK FOR: Tiny, colorless, steeply pointed four-sided crystals in little clusters within cavities in basalt

SIZE: Individual crystals are rarely as long as an eighth of an inch; crystal clusters are occasionally larger, but not by much

COLOR: Colorless to white

OCCURRENCE: Very rare

NOTES: Named for its discoverer, tschernichite is a relatively "new" mineral, discovered in 1991 near Goble, Oregon. This makes it an Oregon type mineral; this means that the mineral was first found in Oregon. Tschernichite is also a zeolite—a member of the group of chemically complex, water-bearing minerals that form within basalt as it is altered by alkaline groundwater. Tschernichite's distinctive crystal shape and extremely rare occurrence easily distinguishes it from all other zeolites. Tschernichite crystals are virtually always colorless and water-clear, and when found individually they exhibit four tapering sides that meet at the top like an elongated pyramid, often with a flattened tip. You'll need a microscope to identify tschernichite, however, as its crystals are typically just hundredths of an inch in size and impossible to identify with the naked eye. Until more closely inspected, it's possible that you'd confuse tschernichite with other glassy clear zeolites like phillipsite (page 197). Aggregates of tschernichite crystals arranged into beautiful radial rosette-like groupings are common as well, making for extremely desirable specimens. Finally, tschernichite often grows upon clay minerals.

WHERE TO LOOK: Road cuts in basalt west of the town of Goble in Columbia County, Oregon, are the only known locality.

Glossary

AGGREGATE: An accumulation or mass of crystals

ALKALINE: Describes substances containing alkali elements, such as calcium, sodium and potassium; having the opposite properties of acid

ALTER: Chemical changes within a rock or mineral due to the addition of mineral solutions

AMPHIBOLE: A large group of important rock-forming minerals commonly found in granite and similar rocks

ASBESTIFORM: Having the qualities of asbestos

ASBESTOS: A very fibrous, flexible, silky-feeling mineral formation; it can refer to several different minerals; due to the possibility of loose, airborne fibers, asbestos minerals pose an inhalation danger

ASSOCIATED: Minerals that often occur together due to similar chemical traits

ASTHENOSPHERE: A layer of the earth's interior that consists of magma and exists beneath the lithosphere

BAND: An easily identified layer within a mineral

BED: A large, flat mass of rock, generally sedimentary

BOTRYOIDAL: Crusts of a mineral that formed in rounded masses, resembling a bunch of grapes

BRECCIA: A coarse-grained rock composed of broken angular rock fragments solidified together

CHALCEDONY: A massive, microcrystalline variety of quartz

CLEAVAGE: The property of a mineral to break along the planes of its crystal structure, which reflects its internal crystal shape

COMPACT: Dense, tightly formed rocks or minerals

CONCENTRIC: Circular, ringed bands that share the same center, with larger rings encompassing smaller rings

CONTINENTAL PLATE: A tectonic plate beneath a continent or other major landform; crust is typically granite

CONCHOIDAL: A rounded shape resembling a half-moon, generally referring to fracture

CRUST: The rigid outermost layer of the earth

CRYSTAL: A solid body with a repeating atomic structure formed when an element or chemical compound solidifies

CUBIC: A box-like structure with sides of an equal size

DEHYDRATE: To lose water contained within

DETRITUS: Debris, especially plant matter

DRUSE: A coating of small crystals on the surface of another rock or mineral

DULL: A mineral that is poorly reflective

EARTHY: Resembling soil; dull luster and rough texture

EFFERVESCE: When a mineral placed in an acid gives off bubbles caused by the mineral dissolving

EPITAXIAL: A mineral growth occurring on the surfaces of another mineral while retaining the underlying mineral's crystal shape

ERUPTION: The ejection of volcanic materials (lava, ash, etc.) onto the earth's surface

FELDSPAR: An extremely common and diverse group of light-colored minerals that are most prevalent within rocks and make up the majority of the earth's crust

FIBROUS: Fine, rod-like crystals that resemble cloth fibers

FLUORESCENCE: The property of a mineral to give off visible light when exposed to ultraviolet light radiation

FRACTURE: The way a mineral breaks or cracks when struck, often referred to in terms of shape or angles

GLACIER: Immense sheets and rivers of slow-moving ice, sometimes over a mile thick, that scour the earth

GLASSY: A mineral with a reflectivity similar to window glass, also known as "vitreous luster"

GNEISS: A rock that has been metamorphosed so that some of its minerals are aligned in parallel bands

GRANITIC: Pertaining to granite or granite-like rocks

GRANULAR: A texture or appearance of rocks or minerals that consist of grains or particles

HEXAGONAL: A six-sided structure

HOST: A rock or mineral on or in which other rocks and minerals occur

HYDROUS: Containing water

ICE AGE: A period of low temperatures worldwide, the last of which ended approximately 10,000 years ago

IGNEOUS ROCK: Rock resulting from the cooling and solidification of molten rock material, such as magma or lava

IMPURITY: A foreign mineral within a host mineral that often changes properties of the host, particularly color

INCLUSION: A mineral that is encased or impressed into a host mineral

IRIDESCENCE: When a mineral exhibits a rainbow-like play of color

LAVA: Molten rock that has reached the earth's surface

LITHOSPHERE: A solid layer directly beneath the earth's outer crust that is divided into pieces called tectonic plates

LUSTER: The way in which a mineral reflects light off of its surface, described by its intensity

MAGMA: Molten rock that remains deep within the earth

MASSIVE: Mineral specimens found not as individual crystals but rather as solid, compact concentrations; rocks are often described as massive; in geology, "massive" is rarely used in reference to size

MATRIX: The rock in which a mineral forms

METAMORPHIC ROCK: Rock derived from the alteration of existing igneous or sedimentary rock through the forces of heat and pressure

METAMORPHOSED: A rock or mineral that has already undergone metamorphosis

MICA: A large group of minerals that occur as thin flakes arranged into layered aggregates resembling a book

MICROCRYSTALLINE: Crystal structure too small to see with the naked eye

MINERAL: A naturally occurring chemical compound or native element that solidifies with a definite internal crystal structure

NATIVE ELEMENT: An element found naturally uncombined with any other elements, e.g. copper

NODULE: A rounded mass consisting of a mineral, generally formed within a vesicle

OCEANIC PLATE: A tectonic plate beneath an ocean; crust is typically basalt

OCTAHEDRAL: A structure with eight-faces, resembling two pyramids placed base-to-base

OPAQUE: Material that lets no light through

ORE: Rocks or minerals from which metals can be extracted

OXIDATION: The process of a metal or mineral combining with oxygen, which can produce new colors or minerals

PEARLY: A mineral with reflectivity resembling that of a pearl

PHENOCRYST: A crystal embedded within igneous rock that solidified before the rest of the surrounding rock, thus retaining its true crystal shape

PLACER: Deposit of sand containing dense, heavy mineral grains at the bottom of a river or a lake

PORPHYRY: An igneous rock containing many phenocrysts

PRISMATIC: Crystals with a length greater than their width

PSEUDOMORPH: When one mineral replaces another but retains the outward appearance of the initial mineral

PYROXENE: A group of hard, dark, rock-building minerals that make up many dark-colored rocks like basalt or gabbro

RADIATING: Crystal aggregates growing outward from a central point, often resembling the shape of a paper fan

RHOMBOHEDRON: A six-sided shape resembling a tilted or leaning cube

ROCK: A massive aggregate of mineral grains

ROCK-BUILDER: Refers to a mineral important in rock creation

SCHILLER: Unusual metallic or iridescent appearance within some minerals, caused by tiny internal growths of other minerals; schiller often intensifies with side-to-side movement of specimen

SCHIST: A rock that has been metamorphosed so that most of its minerals have been concentrated and arranged into parallel layers

SEDIMENT: Fine particles of rocks or minerals deposited by water or wind, e.g. sand

SEDIMENTARY ROCK: Rock derived from sediment being cemented together

SERIES: A group of minerals with nearly identical chemical compositions wherein one element can freely interchange with another and retain the same crystal structure

SILICA: Silicon dioxide; forms quartz when pure and crystallized, and contributes to thousands of minerals

SPECIFIC GRAVITY: The ratio of the density of a given solid or liquid to the density of water when the same amount of each is used, e.g. the specific gravity of copper is approximately 8.9, meaning that a sample of copper is about 8.9 times heavier than the same volume of water

SPECIMEN: A sample of a rock or mineral

STALACTITE: A cone-shaped mineral deposit grown downward from the roof of a cavity; sometimes described as icicle-shaped; formations in this shape are said to be stalactitic

STRATOVOLCANO: A cone-shaped volcano composed of layers of lava and ash produced during past eruptions

STRIATED: Parallel grooves in the surface of a mineral

SUBDUCTION: The process of one tectonic plate descending beneath another; typically occurs to an oceanic plate

SUBDUCTION ZONE: A long, narrow region along a tectonic plate's boundary where subduction takes place

TABULAR: A crystal structure in which one dimension is notably shorter than the others, resulting in flat, plate-like shapes

TECTONIC PLATE: A rigid segment of the lithosphere that is able to move and adjoins other tectonic plates

TARNISH: A thin coating on the surface of a metal, often differently colored than the metal itself (see *oxidation*)

TRANSLUCENT: A material that lets some light through

TRANSPARENT: A material you can see through

TRENCH: A long depression formed at a subduction zone

TWIN: An intergrowth of two or more crystals

VEIN: A mineral, particularly a metal, that has filled a crack or similar opening in a host rock or mineral

VESICLE/VESICULAR: A cavity created in an igneous rock by a gas bubble trapped when the rock solidified; a rock containing vesicles is said to be vesicular

VOLCANO: An opening, or vent, in the earth's surface that allows volcanic material such as lava and ash to erupt

WAXY: A mineral with a reflectivity resembling that of wax

ZEOLITE: A group of similar minerals with very complex chemical structures that include elements such as sodium, calcium and aluminum that are combined with silica and water; zeolites typically form within cavities in basalt as it is affected by mineral-bearing alkaline groundwater

Washington Rock Shops and Museums

BURKE MUSEUM OF NATURAL HISTORY AND CULTURE
University of Washington
17th Ave NE and NE 45th Street
Seattle, WA 98195
www.burkemuseum.org

EARTHLIGHT GEMS & MINERALS
46 Lakeshore Plaza
Kirkland, WA 98033
(425) 828-3872
www.earthlightgems.com

ELLENSBURG AGATE & BEAD SHOP
201 S Main Street
Ellensburg, WA 98926
(509) 925-4998

HANDLEY ROCK & JEWELRY SUPPLY
6160 Highway 99
Vancouver, WA 98665
(503) 292-7990
www.handleyrockandjewelry.com

JERRY'S ROCK & GEM
804 West Valley Highway
Kent, WA 98032
(253) 852-0539

WASHINGTON STATE UNIVERSITY GEOLOGY MUSEUMS
(3 museums) Pullman Campus
Pullman, WA 99163
www.sees.wsu.edu/Museums/index.html

WOOLLY MAMMOTH ROCK SHOP
255341 Highway 101
Port Angeles, WA 98362
(360) 417-8036

Oregon Rock Shops and Museums

AL & MERLE'S ROCK SHOP
28816 Highway 34
Corvallis, OR 97333
(541) 752-5085

CANUTT'S GEMS
7840 S Highway 97
Redmond, OR 97756
(541) 548-2333

ED'S HOUSE OF GEMS
7712 NE Sandy Boulevard
Portland, OR 97213
(503) 284-8990

ELKINS GEMSTONES
972 S Main Street
Prineville, OR 97754
(541) 447-5547

FACETS GEM & MINERAL GALLERY (rock shop)
1240 NW Grove Street
Newport, OR 97365
(541) 265-2514

JAILHOUSE ROCKS (rock shop)
570 2nd Street SE
Bandon, OR 97411
(541)347-7625

Oregon Rock Shops and Museums *(continued)*

JOHN DAY FOSSIL BEDS NATIONAL MONUMENT
www.nps.gov/joda/index.htm
(541) 987-2333

RICE NORTHWEST MUSEUM OF ROCKS & MINERALS
26385 NW Groveland Drive
Hillsboro, OR 97124
(503) 647-2418
www.ricenorthwestmuseum.org

RICHARDSON'S ROCK RANCH (fee digging and rock shop)
6683 NE Haycreek Road
Madras, OR 97741
(541) 475-2680
www.richardsonrockranch.com

RIVERVIEW GEMS & GIFTS
125B Baltimore Ave SE
Bandon, OR 97411
(541) 347-9715

Bibliography and Recommended Reading

Books about Washington and Oregon Minerals

Alt, David D. and Hyndman, Donald W. *Roadside Geology of Oregon*. Missoula: Mountain Press Publishing Company, 1978.

Alt, David D. and Hyndman, Donald W. *Roadside Geology of Washington*. Missoula: Mountain Press Publishing Company, 1994.

Romain, Garret. *Gem Trails of Oregon*. Baldwin Park: Gem Guides Book Company, 1989.

Romain, Garret. *Gem Trails of Washington*. Baldwin Park: Gem Guides Book Company, 2007.

Rygle, Kathy J. and Pederson, Stephen F. *Northwest Treasure Hunter's Gem & Mineral Guide*. Woodstock: Gemstone Press, 2011.

Bibliography and Recommended Reading *(continued)*

General Reading

Bates, Robert L., editor. *Dictionary of Geological Terms, 3rd Edition*. New York: Anchor Books, 1984.

Bonewitz, Ronald Louis. *Smithsonian Rock and Gem*. New York: DK Publishing, 2005.

Chesteman, Charles W. *The Audubon Society Field Guide to North American Rocks and Minerals*. New York: Knopf, 1979.

Johnsen, Ole. *Minerals of the World*. New Jersey: Princeton University Press, 2004.

Mottana, Annibale, et al. *Simon and Schuster's Guide to Rocks and Minerals*. New York: Simon and Schuster, 1978.

Pellant, Chris. *Rocks and Minerals*. New York: Dorling Kindersley Publishing, 2002.

Pough, Frederick H. *Rocks and Minerals*. Boston: Houghton Mifflin, 1988.

Index

About the Authors

Dan R. Lynch has a degree in graphic design with emphasis on photography from the University of Minnesota Duluth. But before his love of art and writing came a passion for rocks and minerals, developed during his lifetime growing up in his parents' rock shop in Two Harbors, Minnesota. Combining the two aspects of his life seemed a natural choice and he enjoys researching, writing about, and taking photographs of rocks and minerals. Working with his father, Bob Lynch, a respected veteran of Lake Superior's agate-collecting community, Dan spearheads their series of rock and mineral field guides—definitive guidebooks that help amateurs "decode" the complexities of geology and mineralogy. He also takes special care to ensure that his photographs compliment the text and always represent each rock or mineral exactly as it appears in person. Encouraged by his wife, Julie, he works as a writer and photographer.

Bob Lynch is a lapidary and jeweler living and working in Two Harbors, Minnesota. He has been cutting and polishing rocks and minerals since 1973, when he desired more variation in gemstones for his work with jewelry. When he moved from Douglas, Arizona, to Two Harbors in 1982, his eyes were opened to Lake Superior's entirely new world of minerals. In 1992, Bob and his wife Nancy, whom he taught the art of jewelry making, acquired Agate City Rock Shop, a family business founded by Nancy's grandfather, Art Rafn, in 1962. Since the shop's revitalization, Bob has made a name for himself as a highly acclaimed agate polisher and as an expert resource for curious collectors seeking advice. Now, the two jewelers keep Agate City Rocks and Gifts open year-round and are the leading source for Lake Superior agates, with more on display and for sale than any other shop in the country.

Notes